I0759553

TO LUCIA AND
ALMA-LUISA WHO
INSPIRED IT ALL

MAKE YOUR OWN ANIMAL FRIENDS

10 Cute Cloth Dolls to Sew, Dress Up and Personalize

KATIA FERRIS

Photography by Susan Bell

Illustrations by Claire Robertson

Quadrille, Penguin Random House UK, One Embassy Gardens, 8 Viaduct Gardens, London SW11 7BW

Quadrille Publishing Limited is part of the Penguin Random House group of companies whose addresses can be found at global.penguinrandomhouse.com

Published by Quadrille in 2025

www.penguin.co.uk
A CIP catalogue record for this book is available from the British Library

ISBN 978 1 83783 294 1
10 9 8 7 6 5 4 3 2 1

Managing Director Sarah Lavelle
Editorial Director Harriet Butt
Design and Art Direction Gemma Hayden
Photography Susan Bell
Prop Stylist Charlie Phillips
Step Illustrations Claire Robertson
Template Illustrations Sarah Fisher
Dog Model Minnie
Head of Production Stephen Lang
Production Manager Sabeena Atchia

Colour reproduction by F1

Printed in China by C&C Offset Printing Co. Ltd

The authorized representative in the EEA is Penguin Random House Ireland, Morrison Chambers, 32 Nassau Street, Dublin D02 YH68.

Penguin Random House is committed to a sustainable future for our business, our readers and our planet. This book is made from Forest Stewardship Council® certified paper.

contents

PATTERNS

See the inside cover at the front and back of this book for the following patterns: ***Owl, Kitty*** and ***Fox***

introduction

I did not grow up sewing, although in my memory it was always around me. When my aunt or grandmother came to stay with us, their visits revolved around the sewing machine and trips to Calico Corners, our local fabric shop. I loved nothing more than to play quietly while listening to them excitedly planning projects, laughing, sewing clothes and making items for our home – curtains, pillows, bedding, so many lovely things. My aunt Conchy sewed beautiful dresses for my sister and me, some of which were worn years later by my daughters and have since been passed down to a younger cousin. They're still perfect.

I regret that I did not learn to sew from Conchy or my grandmother but alas, adults did not have much patience for curious children in those days. So it wasn't until several decades later, when I had daughters of my own and a desire to make them handmade "lovies" for Christmas one year, that I finally taught myself to sew with a borrowed sewing machine and the generous help of many, many YouTube videos and blog tutorials. Through trial and error I learned, little by little, wonky lovie after wonky lovie, year after year. I'm still learning today – on the same sewing machine borrowed from my mother-in-law those many years ago. (Thank you Ginger!)

A "lovie" or a "stuffie" is what my daughters called their stuffed animals, and if I'm not a lifelong sewist, I am certainly a lifelong lover of stuffed animals. Like so many children, my stuffed animals were, to me, fully alive with big feelings and personalities. I didn't have pets growing up, and I was quite a solitary child despite having siblings, so my stuffed animals were very important to me. I invented whole worlds for us.

My first foray into doll-making was when my daughters were three and six. Using an online tutorial, I sewed two kitty dolls, one for each child, out of a pair of polka-dot socks. My daughters named them Dotty and Coco; they were sisters, of course. From that moment on we were all obsessed. Lucia designed and sewed her own bunny lovie, while Alma-Luisa, not yet trusted to wield a needle on her own, would draw wonderful animals on paper, cut them out in a circle with a matching backing, staple them together along their edges and stuff them with crumpled bits of paper to make a stuffie. So creative! A monkey, an elephant, more kitties… our first dolls, were very "kids crafty". Lots of hot glue, buttons, fabric markers and googly eyes. These were wonderfully fun and creative days.

My children eventually moved on to other interests but I had fallen head over heels in love with the process of doll-making.* Not knowing "the right way" to make a doll, I experimented and used whatever materials I had on hand, even if they were unconventional. I just wanted to combine colors, patterns and textures – fabrics I picked up at our local creative re-use store – to create something beautiful and lovable and unbearably cute. There was such freedom in being self-taught and in being a beginner with no rules to hold me back. There was excitement in the challenge and discovery. At times there was frustration as well, but having two little girls/cheerleaders who adored absolutely everything I made, no matter how odd, was very encouraging.

What I have learned in the many years since then, is that there really is no "right way" to make dolls. From Alma-Luisa's stapled stuffies, to simple rag dolls, to the most complicated, jointed art dolls, there are countless ways to make a doll and this book couldn't even begin to cover them all. However, the patterns in this book are designed to give you a sampling of several different approaches to cloth doll-making, from quite simple to more involved.

The patterns in the first section use a basic construction technique and will take you through a variety of methods for adding detail to your doll. Sections 2 and 3 focus on adding depth and dimension to the designs and the last section has patterns for clothing which can be mixed and matched to make a whole wardrobe for the dolls, with lots of options and accessories to play with. Throughout the book, there are also tips for adapting patterns and developing your own designs.

My dearest hope is that you will find this book useful and delightful. I have tried to make it equally engaging whether you are looking at it as a book of patterns to make for yourself or gift, coming to it as an aspiring designer, or as a doll-maker hoping to explore new approaches or find inspiration.

May you find joy in the process and may the lovies you make be treasured and loved.

*I use the terms doll and doll-making in this book, but for me, from day one I wanted to make animals – like the stuffed animals I loved growing up and the pets I always wished I'd had. Not dolls, animals. However, I did want to dress them up like dolls and sew them little things to wear. So, the lovies I make are a sort of hybrid, not truly a doll (not being human) but not truly a stuffed animal either (not having animal bodies or being made of plush fabric or faux fur). Nevertheless, for the sake of simplicity, I'll be using the term "doll" to describe this combination of the best of both worlds, and by extension the term "doll-making" to describe the process of their creation.

getting started

Doll-making can be simple and spontaneous, or it can be very detailed and even, to be honest, sort of fiddly – all those little pattern pieces to keep track of and small arms and legs to turn right side out. There may be many steps that must be done in a very specific order. Take the time to do things the right way, double check the instructions before proceeding, align your pieces correctly, pin pieces together carefully, take a deep breath and sew. Your patience and attention will be well rewarded.

MATERIALS

FABRIC FOR DOLL-MAKING

Choosing the right fabric for doll-making will go a long way in determining your success with a project and in making the process more enjoyable. Look for a medium-weight, woven fabric that has a tight, even weave without too much stretchiness. Here are some suggestions:

- ***Linen blends*** – Cotton-linen blend is my favorite material to use for doll-making. It has wonderful texture and weight
- ***Muslin*** – Use a high-quality, high thread count 100% cotton muslin
- ***Cotton quilting fabric*** – Use a high-quality, high thread count 100% cotton fabric
- ***Cotton flannel*** – If you can find a high-quality, medium-weight flannel, it can make for a wonderful, softly textured doll but be aware that most flannels found in stores tend to be thin and of lower quality

A NOTE ABOUT LINEN

Medium-weight linen can be used if it has a tight weave, but its fluidity and easily fraying raw edges can make linen challenging to work with. In addition, it's quite expensive.

A linen blend is a better option. However, if you choose to use 100% linen, consider using an iron-on fabric stabilizer to make it sturdier and easier to work with.

SOME UNCONVENTIONAL OPTIONS

If you're a beginner, I recommend sticking to the tried-and-true fabrics above. But, if you and your sewing machine have been around the block a few times, you might consider trying a new aisle at your local fabric shore and see what you turn up. I'm a big believer in experimentation! It keeps things fresh and exciting, and can make your work feel more original, although you most certainly do run the risk of adding a degree of difficulty or frustration to your project. The main considerations are weight and stretchiness.

Too light or too stretchy, and the fabric will not be strong enough to withstand stuffing. Too thick or stiff, and it will make turning small arms and legs very unfun. It's also risky to mix different types of fabric on a doll body, because they will stretch at different rates when you stuff them and could make for a misshapen or lumpy (but of course still loveable) doll. But you could consider, for instance, using one of the unconventional options listed below for the body only (which will be easier to turn right side out) and sticking with medium-weight fabric for limbs.

- ***Light-weight canvas***
- ***Light-weight denim***
- ***Twill/brushed twill*** – Brushed twill has a wonderful soft, fuzzy texture but is very sturdy
- ***Corduroy*** – Opt for medium-weight 100% cotton without stretch

FABRIC FOR DETAILS

- ***Wool felt for appliqué*** – If you can afford it, I highly recommend using 100% wool felt. As a natural material, it's lovely to use on children's toys and its quality is unsurpassed. It's soft, durable and heat-resistant, which means it can be ironed. Wool-blend felt is less expensive and can be an acceptable alternative. It can usually be ironed at a low setting. I do not recommend using synthetic or acrylic felt, however, also called craft felt. It's thin and pills, making your doll look worn very quickly. Because it can shed and stretch out of shape easily, it is also more difficult to get a clean edge when cutting it and is generally more difficult to work with. Synthetic felt should not be ironed as it may melt.
- ***Minky, Plush, Fleece, or similar*** – These fabrics are generally too stretchy for the types of dolls we'll be making in this book, but their soft texture makes them perfect for details like ears that won't be stuffed.

MATERIAL FOR CLOTHING

Here is where you can use lighter-weight and more flowy fabrics, which have a lovely drape, for dresses and skirts. If you're a beginner, lighter-weight fabrics can be a bit more challenging to work with. You can also use any of the medium-weight fabrics listed previously. For doll clothing, I suggest the following:

- ***Light-weight linen***
- ***Cotton lawn***
- ¼in (6mm) wide elastic
- ¼in (6mm) wide ribbon or twill tape (optional)
- Lace for detail (optional)

INTERFACING

- ***Woven iron-on interfacing*** – Interfacing adds support and stability to your fabric and minimizes stretchability. It can also help to keep dark embroidery floss (thread) from showing through light-colored fabric. It comes in several different weights and materials – choose one that is of a similar weight to your fabric or slightly lighter. As its name suggests, the interfacing is ironed onto the back/wrong side of your fabric (see Owl on pages 54–58 for an illustration).

EMBROIDERY FLOSS (THREAD) AND CORDS

- Embroidery floss comes in a huge variety of colors. It's made up of six strands of embroidery thread, usually cotton, which are loosely twisted together and designed to be separated. By varying the number of strands used, you can change the thickness of your stitching. I use three strands the majority of the time, but may switch to two strands for more delicate or nuanced stitching, or use more than three strands when I want bolder stitching.
- *Cord or twine in any material is used for the Mouse's tail (see page 82)* – cotton macramé cording or leather cord work well.

STUFFING

While there are several types of stuffing that work well for doll-making, unfortunately the natural options such as wool, bamboo or cotton can be difficult to find and significantly more expensive. I use polyester fiber fill which is widely available, inexpensive, easy to use and retains its shape over time.

SAFETY CONSIDERATIONS

It's extremely important to consider safety when designing or making dolls for young children. Keep these guidelines and tips in mind and err on the side of caution.

- Select age-appropriate projects and, if necessary, adapt the instructions to use safe materials and construction methods.
- Use non-toxic, durable materials.
- For children under three years old, any small parts that could come off or out of a doll present a choking hazard, so rethink doll clothing and accessories.
- Avoid using buttons, beads, filler pellets or beans, or plastic eyes and noses. If necessary, adapt projects to use safe materials. For instance, doll eyes can be embroidered in place of using plastic doll eyes.
- Any attached body parts, such as limbs or ears, should be very well secured. From a construction standpoint, it's safest for them to be sewn into a seam and then for that seam to be reinforced with an extra row of stitching.
- Consider leaving off clothing or accessories or alternatively, securely stitching them to the doll. Do not use buttons or snaps.
- Likewise, avoid using long ribbons or strings as they could present a danger of strangulation.
- If in doubt, leave it out.

TOOLS FOR DOLL-MAKING

FOR TRANSFERRING PATTERNS

- Paper
- Pen or pencil
- Tissue paper (optional)
- Disappearing-ink pen
- Ruler
- Freezer paper (optional)

FOR CUTTING

- Scissors for cutting fabric
- Separate pair of scissors for cutting paper
- Pinking shears aka zig-zag scissors
- ¼in (6mm) hole punch for cutting felt circles (optional)

FOR SEWING

- Sewing machine
- Sewing/embroidery needles
- All-purpose thread
- Iron
- Doll needle
- Straight pins
- Extra-strong thread for attaching arms and ladder stitch closure, such as upholstery, button or crochet thread
- Embroidery floss
- Flexible measuring tape
- 5in (12.5cm) embroidery hoop (optional)
- Small safety pin (for threading elastic in some clothing)

FOR TURNING AND STUFFING

- Stuffing
- Hemostat or large tweezers
- Chopstick
- Turning tube (optional)

FOR EMBELLISHING

- Black gel fabric marker (Pentel gel roller pen for fabric)
- Blush, beeswax crayon or pencil for rosy cheeks, optional (see page 32)
- 9mm plastic doll eyes (optional) – the monkey pattern uses doll eyes, but they could be replaced with felt or embroidery
- Awl or ⅛in (3mm) hole punch (optional if using doll eyes, see page 28)

SASHIKO
STOCKMAR
Fine Point Disappearing ink
Gütermann

techniques

Here you will find basic techniques used for the projects in this book and for doll-making in general. Additionally, there are sections throughout the book with more doll-making and designing techniques.

USING PATTERNS

PATTERN MARKINGS

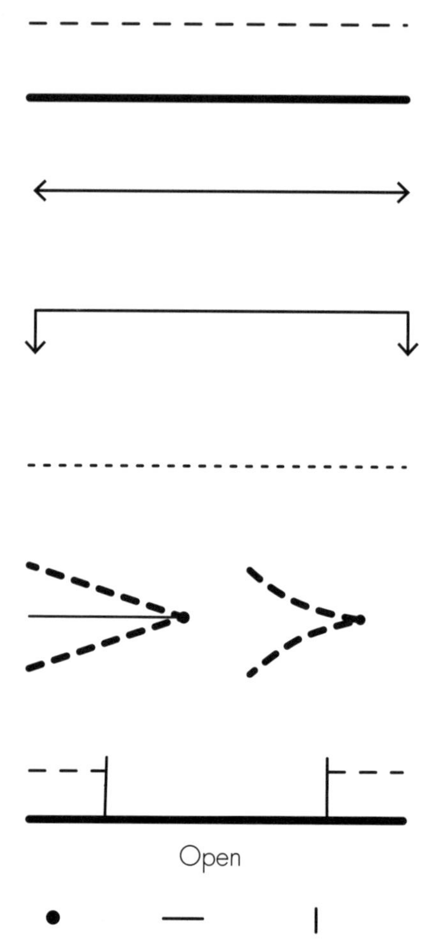

Stitch or *sewing line* – the dashed inner line

Cut or *cutting line* – the solid outer line

Grainline – a double-headed arrow indicates how a pattern piece should be positioned on fabric for cutting. The grainline arrow should run parallel to the selvedge edge of the fabric

Place-on-fold – a double-headed arrow bent at the ends indicates that this edge of the pattern piece should be positioned along the folded edge of the fabric. It also indicates the grainline

Fold or fold under line – a dashed line indicating where to fold a piece after it has been sewn

Dart point – indicated by a dot

Dart legs – a pair of dashed lines beginning at the dart point and spreading out to the edge of the fabric. Dart legs can be straight or curved

Markings for openings – indicate an area which is not sewn, leaving an opening for turning a piece right side out

Match dots and match lines – indicate where to match up two pieces of fabric

Placement markings – indicate where to place elements

Dots – these can also indicate gusset start and end points or pivot points. The pattern instructions will specify how they should be used

UNDERSTANDING GRAIN DIRECTION

Grain refers to the way fabric is woven and it's important in sewing because it affects how the fabric will behave. Most patterns, including the ones in this book, include a grainline marking to guide the layout of pattern pieces when cutting fabric. Each pattern piece should be positioned on the fabric so that the grainline marking runs parallel to the fabric grain.

The grainline runs in the same direction as the selvedge edge. This direction is called the straight grain. Many, but not all patterns, are cut on the straight grain. For a piece cut on the straight grain, the grainline marking on the pattern will be vertical, cross grain is perpendicular to straight grain, running from selvedge edge to selvedge edge. This direction has more stretch. For a piece cut on the cross grain, the pattern will have a horizontal grainline marking. When sewing dolls, it is not advisable to cut fabric diagonally or "on the bias" because it will have too much stretch and may cause odd rippling along the seams.

When designing, a pattern can be laid out on the straight grain or cross grain as long as you are aware that it will affect the outcome of your project. A doll made on the straight grain will be wider, while one made on the cross grain will be taller.

PDF PATTERNS

Scan the QR code to access the pattern downloads for this book using the password Lucky.

All the patterns featured are available to download and print. See page 17 for instructions on how to prepare the patterns to use.

SEAM ALLOWANCE

A ¼in (6mm) seam allowance is included on all doll patterns in this book. Each pattern piece will have two lines; the solid line is the cutting line, which includes the seam allowance, and the dashed inner line marks the stitching line which you should follow when sewing the seams. It is crucial to check the pattern and instructions carefully to determine which line to use. On each pattern piece one of these lines will be bold indicating which line should be copied. This may seem unnecessarily confusing, but there are several reasons why I have chosen to include both lines.

The cutting line is used when fabric pieces need to be cut out before being sewn together. Then when sewing, if your machine has a quarter-inch foot, simply line up the cut edge of the fabric with the outer edge of the presser foot to obtain a ¼in (6mm) seam allowance. If your presser foot is not the correct size, use a piece of masking tape or washi tape on the needle plate to mark where the edge of the fabric should line up in order to obtain a ¼in (6mm) seam allowance. When patterns or pattern books do not include seam allowance that means it must be added in by us. Not only is this time-consuming and tiresome, but if we don't use the right methods or tools to do so, we risk losing precision when cutting out the fabric.

At other times, especially for parts like arms, legs or ears, it is much more efficient to use the stitch line. In this case, the stitch line is transferred to fabric which has been folded with right sides together. You then sew directly on the stitch line without first having to cut out the pieces. This not only saves a step, but also gives us a stitch guide allowing us to be more precise in our sewing. This can be particularly helpful around small curves.

From a design standpoint, modifications to a pattern should always be made to the stitch line rather than to the cutting line. That's because a pattern piece with seam allowance included does not give an accurate sense of its true shape and size. Altering a piece without seam allowance allows us to more easily visualize changes and gives us more accuracy and a better chance of success. Once alterations have been made, add the seam allowance back to the pattern piece using a ruler, seam gauge or French curve.

PREPARING THE PATTERN

1. Trace/photocopy/download the pattern from the book (see page 15, the front- and back-inside cover or the end of the relevant book section). ***All the patterns featured in this book are 100% to scale.*** If you will be using a pattern over and over, consider making it more durable by photocopying the pattern pieces onto card stock or gluing them onto thin cardboard or pasteboard.

2. Cut the pattern out. Always cut on the inside edge of the line so that the pattern maintains its size and shape once traced out on fabric.

3. Label all pattern pieces. On each pattern piece include:

   - Name of pattern, i.e. "Mouse"
   - Name of pattern piece, i.e. "Body"
   - Whether to cut or sew the piece
   - Number of pieces you'll need and whether or not they should be mirrored, i.e. "Cut 1 mirrored pair"
   - Which fabric to use if the project calls for more than one fabric i.e. "Fabric A"
   - Direction of grainline: marked with a double-headed arrow
   - Pattern markings – Use an awl or large needle to make a small hole in the pattern piece for any dot markings. The hole needs to be just large enough for the tip of a marking tool to fit through and mark the fabric underneath. For markings along the edge of a pattern such as match lines or markings for openings, make an ⅛in (3mm) long snip at the edge of the piece; you will be able to mark the fabric through the slit.

TRANSFERRING THE PATTERN TO FABRIC

This requires a good marking tool. I recommend a disappearing-ink pen. The marks should fully disappear in 2–3 days or can be removed sooner with water. It's always a good idea to test any marking tool on the fabric you'll be using to ensure the markings will completely disappear.

LAYING OUT PATTERN PIECES

- Check the instructions to determine whether to transfer each pattern piece to a single or double layer of fabric. To obtain a pair of mirrored pieces, you will be directed to lay the pattern piece onto fabric which has been folded with right sides together.
- Place each pattern piece on the wrong side of the fabric, matching the grainline arrow on the pattern to the grain of the fabric.
- Lay out pieces as economically as possible.
- For pattern pieces that do not include a seam allowance, make sure to leave ample space surrounding each piece.

TRACING THE OUTLINE

Hold or pin each pattern piece in place while you trace the outline onto the wrong side of the fabric. I generally transfer all pattern markings to the wrong side of the fabric first when tracing the outline. Then, I add any markings that need to be on the right side of the fabric, transferring them after the piece, or pieces for doubled fabric, have been cut out, using one of the following methods.

DIRECT MARKING

For this method, simply flip over the fabric piece so that the right side is facing up, lay the pattern piece over it, and transfer the markings. For pieces that are not symmetrical, you would also need to flip over the pattern piece in order to position it correctly over the fabric piece. For patterns transferred to doubled fabric, open up the fabric pieces so that both are laying with right sides facing up, line up the pattern piece over each fabric piece and transfer markings to right sides, flipping the pattern piece over once for non-symmetrical pieces.

PIN METHOD

A more precise method to transfer markings to the right side of a piece is the pin method. Insert a pin directly through the center of the marking on the wrong side of the fabric; on the right side of the fabric, use a disappearing-ink pen to mark the spot where the pin has emerged.

To use this method for pieces which have been cut from doubled fabric, first be sure the two fabric pieces are lined up carefully, then insert a pin through the marking on the wrong side of the top piece so that it pierces both layers of fabric (see illustration A). It's best if the pieces are laying on a flat surface to ensure that the pin goes in straight and perpendicular to the surface. To transfer a marking to the right sides of both pieces, gently fold back the top fabric piece without pulling the pin out of the bottom piece and mark the spots where the pin has pierced the fabric pieces (see illustration B). To transfer a marking to the wrong side of the second piece, mark the spot where the pin emerges on the wrong side of the bottom piece.

PIN METHOD

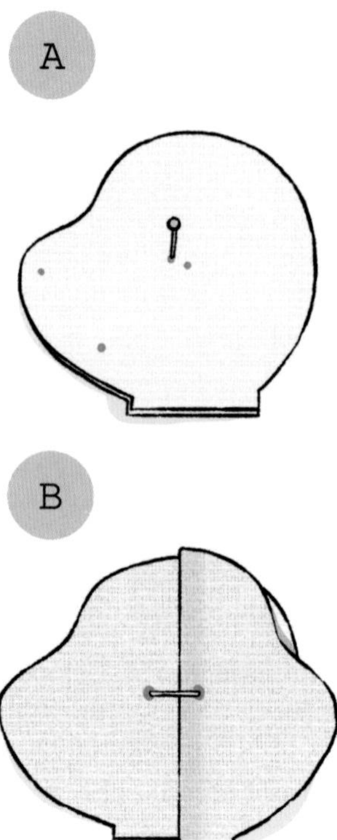

STENCIL METHOD

C

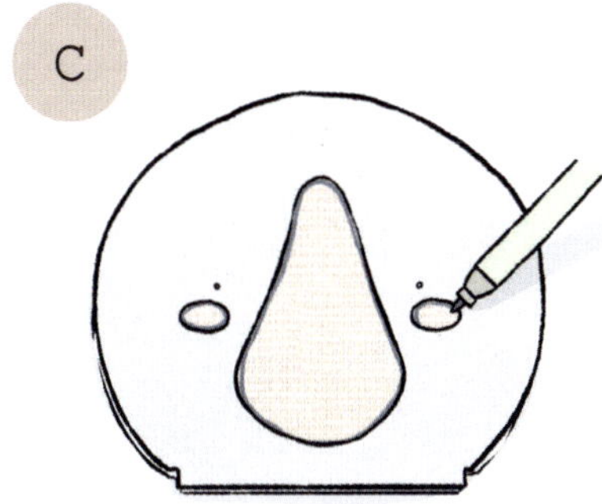

D

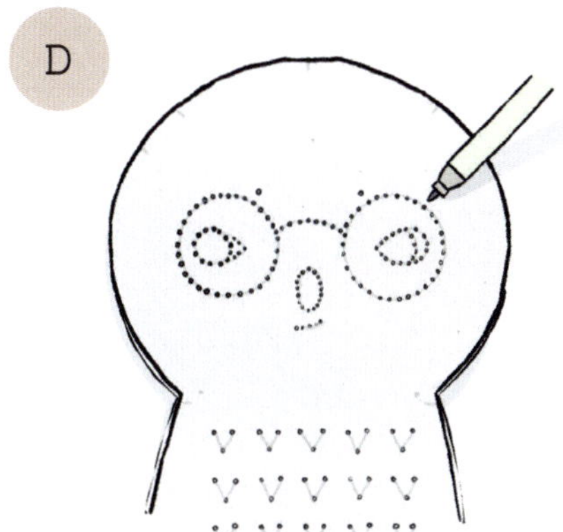

E

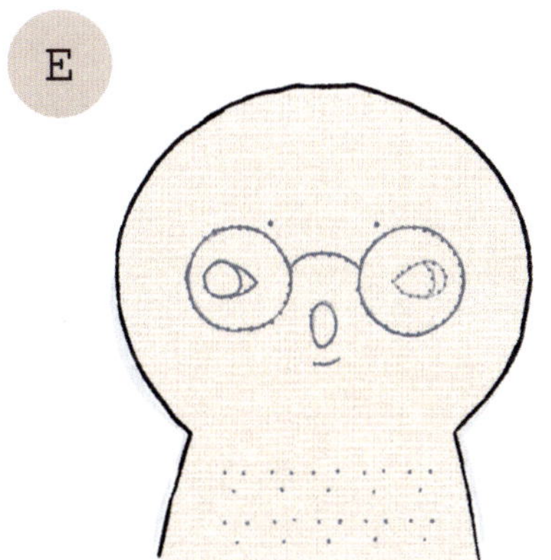

MARKING ON THE DETAILS

For pattern pieces with a lot of detail, such as faces or pieces that will be appliquéd or embroidered, there are several approaches you can take. Once you have cut out your pattern piece, transfer the detailed markings to the right side of the fabric using one of the following methods.

LIGHTBOX OR WINDOW METHOD

This method works well with lighter-colored fabrics. Tape the paper pattern to a window or lightbox. (Keep in mind that your computer screen can function as a lightbox.) Lay the fabric piece on top with the right side facing up. Line it up carefully, then trace the pattern markings with a disappearing-ink pen.

STENCIL METHOD

With this method, the paper pattern is essentially used as a stencil. Cut shapes out of the paper pattern so that you can trace along the inside edge of the hole onto the fabric with a disappearing-ink pen (see illustration C). For linear elements, use an awl or large needle to make small holes in the pattern piece at ⅛in–¼in (3mm–¼in) intervals along a curved line. For straight lines, you only need to make two holes, one at each end of the line. Using a disappearing-ink pen, mark the fabric through the small holes you've made (see illustration D), remove the paper pattern and join the dots to transfer the line(s), (illustration E). For straight lines, use a ruler to connect the dots.

GRID METHOD

With a pencil and ruler, draw out a simple grid on your paper pattern piece. Often just two simple intersecting lines are sufficient, one horizontal and one vertical, through the center of the pattern. On the fabric piece, duplicate these lines. Make sure you have tested the disappearing-ink pen first to ensure the marks will not be permanent. On the paper pattern, one at a time measure the distance of each of the various design elements from the grid lines (i.e. nose, eyes, etc.). You will then know exactly where to place the design elements on your fabric. At this point, you can draw them out freehand directly on your fabric or trace and cut the various elements out of paper, place them using the measurements, and use them as stencils to transfer their outline onto the fabric.

assembly techniques

BASIC SEWING

In this section you will find some basic sewing tips for doll-making. Additional sewing skills are added where appropriate throughout the book.

STITCH LENGTH

Using a short stitch length is very important when making dolls because the stuffing process will put a considerable amount of strain on the seams. Unless otherwise stated in the pattern instructions, I recommend using a stitch length of no more than 2mm, and optimally 1.5mm, but bear in mind that a 1.5mm stitch length will make it quite difficult to remove stitches if a mistake is made.

SECURING SEAMS

Unless otherwise stated in the pattern instructions, backstitch to secure at the beginning and end of every seam. Backstitch 5–6 stitches in order to "lock" stitches and keep seams from unraveling.

REINFORCING SEAMS

I also suggest reinforcing seams at stress points, such as the neck and crotch, and places where appendages are attached, such as arms, legs and ears. To reinforce a seam, sew a second line of stitches over the seam line in the area that you want to reinforce, backstitching at the beginning and end to secure.

BASTING/HAND TACKING

Basting is a very helpful, quick way to temporarily attach something or hold two or more items together. You can think of it as a temporary seam, used when straight pins might be too bulky or get in the way.

Use the Baste function on your sewing machine if it has one. If not, set your machine's stitch length to its longest length, usually 5–6mm, and loosen the tension to 3. Attach pieces using an ⅛in (3mm) seam allowance. Later, you can easily take out the basting stitches with a seam ripper. Hand-tacking is essentially the same as basting only it is done by hand with long running stitches.

BASTING TO GATHER FABRIC

Basting stitches can be used to evenly gather material or make ruffles when sewing garments and accessories. Use the Baste function on your sewing machine with the usual 5–6mm stitch length or, for light-weight fabrics, shorten the stitch length to 4mm. Leaving thread tails long at either end, sew two rows of basting stitches ¼–½in (6mm–1.2cm) apart. Do not backstitch at the beginning and end of the stitch lines. The rows should be parallel to each other and to the edge of the fabric. To gather the fabric, take hold of the bobbin thread tails (the bobbin thread is on the underside). Working from each side towards the center, slide the fabric along the thread to create gathers and distribute them evenly.

CLIPPING CORNERS AND CURVES AND TRIMMING SEAM ALLOWANCES

Once you have sewn your seams, but before turning your work right side out, you must clip the curves and corners on each piece. This is arguably one of the most important steps to give a crisp clean finish to your seams with no puckering or pulling.

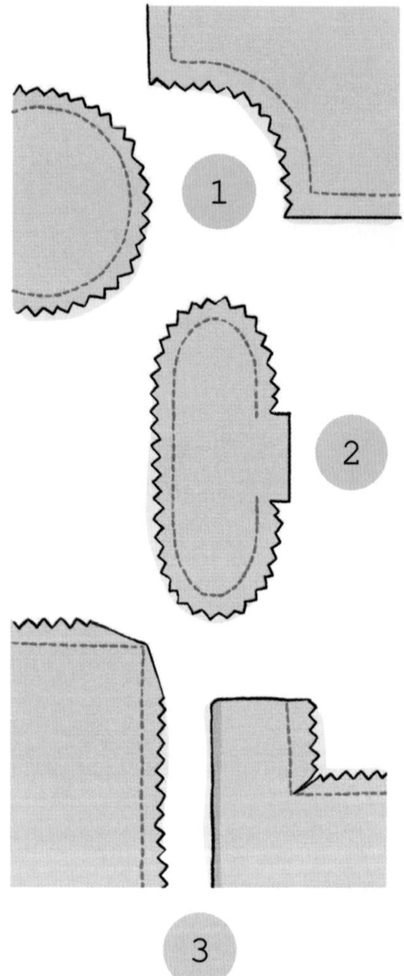

1. *Curves* – On curves, it is recommended to cut V-shaped notches into the seam allowance with the point of the notch coming just to the stitch line without cutting through it. Make notches every ⅛–¼in (3–6mm) or so. This will allow the seam allowance to stretch apart to accommodate the curves. I find that using pinking shears to trim down seam allowances works very well and is a quicker and easier alternative to making individual notches. It also helps to reduce bulk and keep edges from fraying.

2. *Openings* – When trimming the seam allowance on a piece that has an opening for turning, leave the seam allowance at the opening intact/uncut so that later, after you've turned the piece right side out, you can neatly tuck in and press the seam allowance. A crisp, neatly folded edge will make it easier to sew the opening closed.

3. *Corners* – For outward corners, remove excess fabric by cutting diagonally across the tip of the corner as close to the seam line as possible without cutting into it and then tapering the seam allowances on the sides toward the point of the corner. For inward corners, such as at the neck or crotch, clip into the seam allowance by cutting a straight line from the edge of the fabric towards the point of the corner almost all the way to the stitch line without cutting through it. At the crotch you will need to make two or three cuts, one into each of the angles.

PRESSING OPEN SEAMS

This is another step that will help your dolls to look more polished. Unless otherwise indicated in the pattern instructions, after sewing each seam, separate the seam allowances and press them open with an iron or at the very least fingerpress them with your fingernail.

TURNING WORK RIGHT SIDE OUT

This can be one of the most fiddly and frustrating aspects of doll-making when we're dealing with tiny or narrow pieces. Having the right tool can make the process much easier. Start by trimming seam allowances closely to decrease bulk, then try using one of the following tools to turn the work right side out.

Turning tube – Personally, I have found the best success with turning tubes. These typically come in a set of three sizes or can be assembled at home with a straw and a knitting needle or chopstick. Using the widest tube that will fit into the piece, insert the tube through the opening as far as it will go, then use the corresponding stick to gently press the fabric into the tube (see the photograph above). Rather than trying to push the stick down through the tube, instead try to ease the fabric up over the stick. This is especially important when using delicate or loosely woven fabric because of the risk of poking a hole through the piece.

Chopstick – Although more challenging, a chopstick can be used in a similar way if you don't have a turning tube. Pinch apart the fabric furthest from the opening and tuck the seam into the space you've created so that you have a little pocket into which you can insert the chopstick. Brace the bottom of the chopstick against your body to hold it steady as you use both hands to gently guide the fabric over the chopstick.

Hemostat – This can be used like a very long pair of tweezers to reach into the piece, grab onto the fabric furthest from the opening and draw it out.

PRESSING OUT SEAMS

Once the piece has been turned right side out, gently run the tip or side of a chopstick along the inside of each seam to make sure it's pushed out completely, then press well. Take extra care in areas like the tip of the nose, curved areas or where there are bulky seams. For most pieces, you will also need to tuck in the seam allowance at the opening, align the folded edges neatly, then press well to get a crisp crease.

STUFFING

Don't underestimate the importance of good stuffing technique as it will impact both the look and feel of your doll. Add just a little bit of stuffing at a time and take care to work symmetrically. Don't rush it.

1. Gently push a small bunch of filler through the opening using your fingers or a pair of tweezers or a hemostat.

2. Begin by stuffing the furthest point from the opening and then alternate sides, slowly filling in the shape. Use your pointer finger/index finger or thumb to push stuffing into the seams. You may need to use the wide end of a chopstick for long, narrow shapes like arms or legs.

3. Patiently build up filling slowly and evenly until any puckering along the seams is smoothed out.

4. Don't be afraid to squish things into shape, for instance if the head is a bit lopsided. Everything is still quite malleable at this point.

5. The head should be stuffed very firmly. Don't understuff. You will be surprised at how much filler it takes to properly stuff a doll. Think back to your childhood lovies with their wobbly heads. Filler will compress over time, so keep stuffing! An issue I often see with beginner doll-makers is that they don't use enough filler to fully stuff a doll. You can see this in the puckered seams or caved-in looking faces. The body does not need to be packed quite as firmly if you would like your doll to have some squishability for hugging.

6. With that said, it's also important not to stuff to the point where you overstrain the seams. Also, depending on how much stretch your fabric has, you may need to take care not to warp the fabric by overstuffing. There's a sweet spot.

7. Once you've closed the opening it's nearly impossible to reposition the stuffing so make any adjustments before closing up the seam.

8. Use ladder stitch to close the opening (see opposite). Once you've stitched almost all the way across the opening, use tweezers or a hemostat to add more filler around the opening before closing it completely.

LADDER STITCH

Ladder stitch is an essential stitch in doll-making. Sometimes called blind stitch or invisible stitch, it's used to close an opening in a seam that was left for turning and stuffing. If done neatly, it can truly disappear and blend in with the machine-sewn seam. I recommend using extra-strong thread in a color that closely matches your fabric or, if you don't have a match, use a lighter-colored thread.

It helps to press your folded edges crisply before stuffing. This will essentially give you a "line" to follow as you sew. You will be stitching through only one layer of fabric, with your needle entering and exiting the channel between the folded layers of fabric.

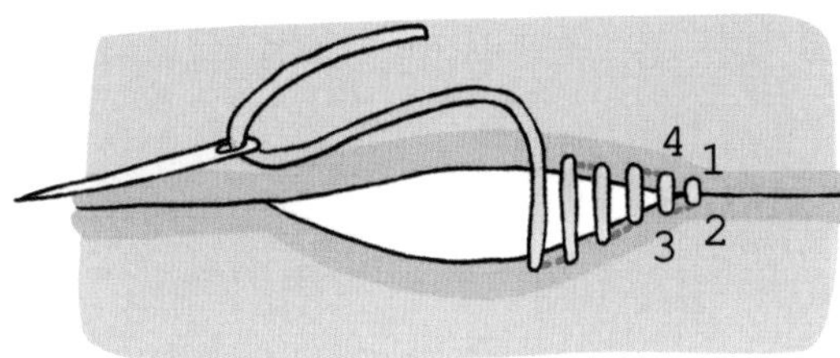

Ladder stitch can also be used to attach body parts to one another. This will be covered later in the book in separate sections:

- Attaching Ears with ladder stitch (see page 86)
- Attaching Head to Body with ladder stitch (see page 100)
- Attaching Legs to Body with ladder stitch (see page 101)

WORKING LADDER STITCH

1. Starting from inside the opening, bring the needle up at 1, just past where the machine-sewn seam ends. Your knot will be hidden on the inside of the doll.

2. Re-insert the needle at 2, directly across from 1. The stitch should be straight and perpendicular to the opening. An angled stitch could cause the fabric to pucker. Make a small stitch ⅛–¼in (3–6mm) long through the channel of the fold, bringing the needle out at 3. Re-insert at 4, again directly across from the previous stitch. Continue making small, even stitches, alternating sides. The smaller your stitches, the more invisible your seam will be.

3. After every few stitches, pull the thread to "close up" the ladder. Be firm but gentle. Pulling too hard can cause the stitches to pucker. Also, take care not to sew too far and then attempt to close up too many stitches at once. The tension could cause the thread to break.

4. Once you've made your way almost all the way across the opening, use tweezers or a hemostat to push bits of stuffing under the already ladder-stitched seam. This is your last opportunity to add stuffing and plump up any hollow-looking areas.

5. When you reach the other side, make a small stitch, bringing your needle up through the machine-sewn seam just past the opening. Leave a loop, then pass your needle through the loop a few times and pull tight to make a knot. Insert your needle down through the seam directly next to the knot, coming out a short distance away. Draw the thread all the way through and tug gently, sinking the knot down into the seam. Trim the thread end close to the fabric and let the tail disappear back into the doll.

ATTACHING ARMS

For most of the dolls in this book, the arms are attached to the body after they have been sewn and stuffed. There are two methods for this, both requiring strong thread and a long doll needle. To begin, position the arms and pin them to the body. It may help to make marks with a disappearing-ink pen on either side of the body and on the arms to use as guides when sewing.

METHOD 1

This is the stronger of the two methods and recommended for dolls that are intended for play. With this method, the attachment is visible as a stitch across the top of the outer arm. This pulls the top of the arms tight against the body creating a sloping transition between neck/body and arm.

1. Cut a long piece of strong thread, at least 62in (157.5cm). Double the thread, knot the ends, insert the doubled end into your needle and draw it through. Trim the tails close to the knot.

2. Following the illustration, insert the needle into the body at 1. Do not draw the thread tight at first. Bring the needle through the body, emerging at 2 and into the underside of the arm, emerging at 3. Make a small stitch across the outside of the arm by re-inserting at 4. Stitch through the arm and into the body at 5. Emerge at 6 and stitch through the underside of the arm, emerging at 7. Make a small stitch across the outside of the arm by re-inserting at 8. Stitch through the arm and back into the body at 1. Emerge at 2. Pull the thread gently but firmly, drawing arms and body together. Repeat these steps once or twice to ensure the arms are securely attached.

3. With the needle emerging between the body and underarm, slip the needle under the stitches and tie off with a strong double knot. For extra security, you can draw the needle back through to the other side of the body and repeat this step on the other side. Re-insert the needle into the body under the arm, emerging further down the torso. Pull firmly to sink the knot and hide it under the arm. Trim thread ends close to the fabric and let them disappear back into the doll.

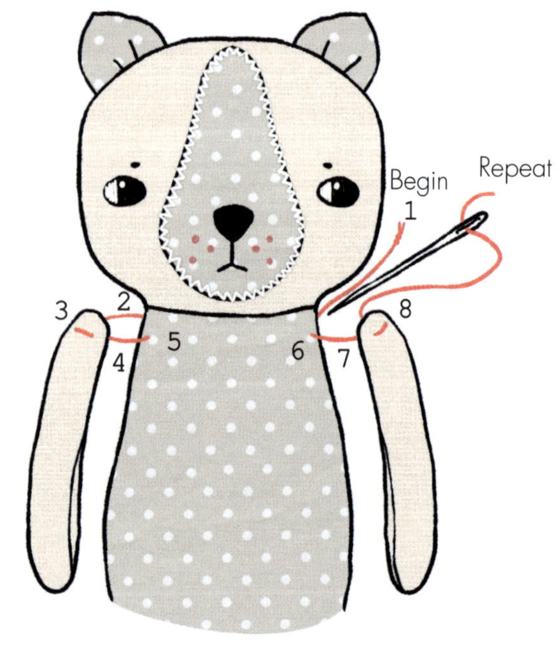

METHOD 2

This method is not as secure as the first, however it does create an invisible attachment. Another difference is that this method does not pull in the tops of the arms, therefore giving more of an impression of shoulders.

1. Cut a long piece of strong thread, at least 45in (114cm). Double the thread, insert the doubled end into the needle and draw it through. Do not knot the ends.

2. Following the illustration, insert the needle into the arm at 1 and emerge at 2. Do not draw the thread all the way through – leave a tail of 4–5in (10–13cm). Note that the stitch goes into and out of the underside of the arm only. Insert the needle into the body at 3, coming out at 4. Insert the needle into the underside of the arm at 5 and emerge on the underside of the arm at 6. Re-insert the needle into the body at 7, coming out at 8.

3. Take the thread off the needle. Holding both ends end of the doubled thread, pull gently but firmly, drawing the arms against the body. Tie off with a strong double knot (see the photograph opposite). Thread one tail end back onto the needle and reinsert under the arm, emerging further down the torso. Pull firmly to sink the knot and hide it under the arm. Trim thread ends close to the fabric and let them disappear back into the doll. Repeat to sink the other end of the doubled thread.

adding detail

DOLL EYES

Plastic doll eyes, also called safety eyes, come in a variety of colors and sizes. They are very easy to use and are a fun way to add character to a doll. Do be aware that, although they are called safety eyes, they pose a choking hazard and are not actually safe for young children. If you prefer not to use doll eyes, swap them out for appliquéd or embroidered eyes.

Doll eyes come in two parts: the eye which is connected to a post, and the washer. Often the post has ridges for the washer to grip onto. You will need a tool in order to poke a small hole in the fabric through which to insert the doll eye. I recommend using an awl or an ⅛in (3mm) hole punch. If you have neither of these, use a small sharp pair of scissors to snip a tiny hole.

1. With disappearing-ink pen, mark the eye placement using the pattern markings. Double check that you're happy with the position and then poke a hole through each marking.
2. Insert the doll eye so that the post comes out on the wrong side of the fabric. With the flat side of the washer facing the fabric, place it over the post and squeeze the washer and doll eye together until you hear a click. The click indicates that the washer is securely fastened. Double check that the washer is secure by trying to pull it off. It should not come off. If it does, flip the washer over and try again. Sometimes with smaller doll eyes, it's hard to tell which is the flat side of the washer, so it's a good idea to double check.
3. For the project in this book, we'll be layering circles of felt under the doll eyes as a design element. If you plan to use doll eyes directly on fabric, I recommend that you sandwich a small scrap of fleece or felt between the wrong side of the fabric and the washer. This will prevent the fabric from puckering and keep the outline of the washer from being visible through the fabric on the front side. Fleece or felt are ideal for this since they are soft and thick. If you're using light-colored fabric, check that the scrap fabric won't show through.

EMBROIDERY STITCHES

Just a handful of basic embroidery stitches are all that's needed to add detail and facial features to a doll. You can think of it as drawing with needle and thread.

STRAIGHT STITCH

The basis for many more complex stitches is one simple stitch.

RUNNING STITCH

A series of evenly spaced straight stitches in a row, a running stitch creates a dashed line or outline.

Bring the needle up through the fabric at 1 and re-insert at 2. Repeat at regular intervals.

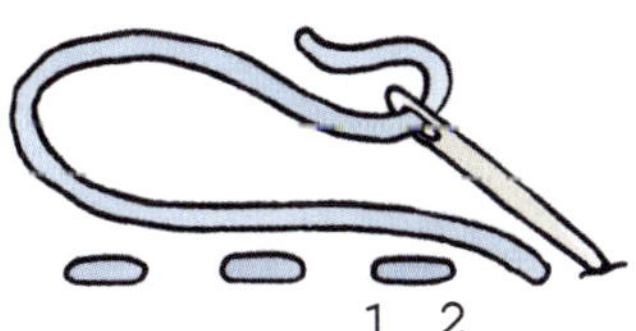

BACKSTITCH

The backstitch creates a solid line and is often used to outline a shape.

Starting one stitch length ahead of where you'd like the stitch or line to begin, bring the needle up at 1. Moving one stitch length backwards, insert the needle at 2. Continue in pattern, bringing the needle up one stitch ahead, at the new point 1.

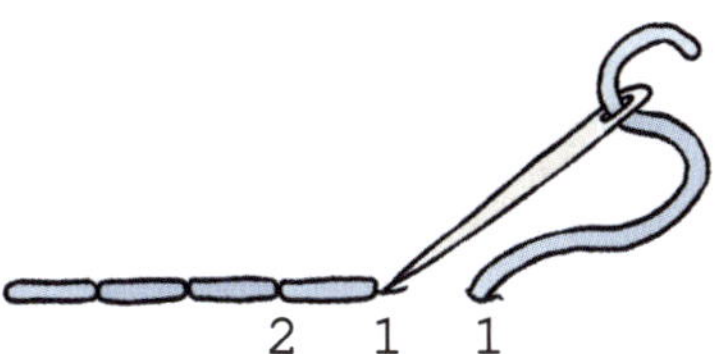

FLY STITCH

The fly stitch can be used to great effect as a grouping or, as a single stitch, it makes a perfect nose. It makes a V- or Y-shape depending on the length of the tacking stitch in the center. A tiny tacking stitch can also allow you to make a stitch with a gentle arc, perfect for a little smile.

Bring the needle up at 1 and re-insert at 2, keeping the stitch loose. Bring the needle up at 3. Draw the working thread under the first stitch then pull gently until taut. For a V-shape, re-insert the needle at 3 tacking the first stitch in place. For a Y-shape, reinsert at 4 further down. The directions for making an arc are the same as for making a V-shape however stitch 3 is placed higher up, centered just below 1 and 2.

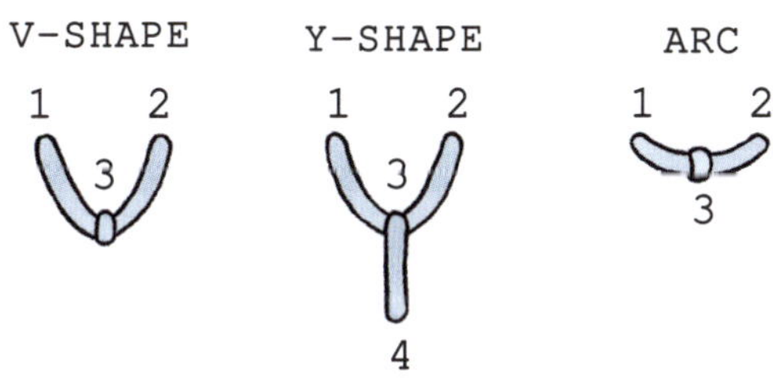

WHIPSTITCH APPLIQUÉ

Whipstitch works nicely as a means to attach a small piece of felt or fabric to a larger piece of fabric by hand. Whipstitch appliqué works particularly well with felt because its edges don't fray. Essentially, it is a series of short even straight stitches worked along the edge of the smaller piece. Tiny whipstitches can almost disappear, while larger stitches or contrasting thread can add a decorative element.

The key to whipstitch appliqué is to maintain an even stitch length as well as a consistent distance between stitches. Stitch length is typically in the range of ⅛–¼in (3–6mm) but can vary based on the scale of the piece. When used for doll-making, closely spaced stitching is recommended so that it will be able to withstand stuffing and play.

Bring the needle up through both layers of fabric at 1, ⅛–¼in (3–6mm) from the edge of the top piece. Re-insert just past the edge of the top piece and into the bottom piece, at 2. Continue in pattern.

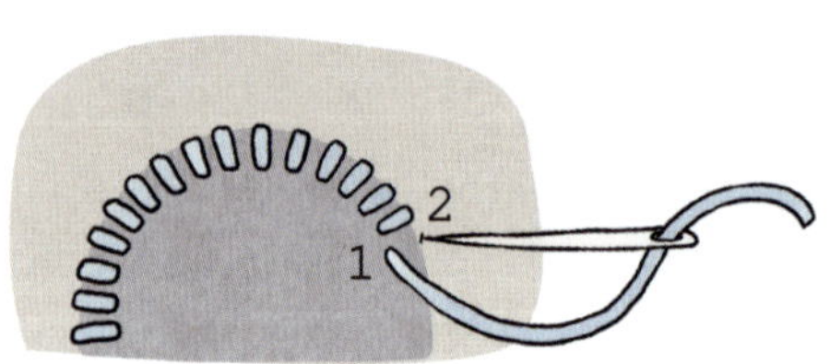

FRENCH KNOT

A fun and versatile stitch, French knots can be used to make, for example, whisker dots, simple eyes on a small doll or to add highlights in more detailed eyes.

You will need both hands to sew a French knot so lay your fabric or doll flat on a table or in your lap. Bring the needle up at 1 (see illustration below). With your other hand, hold the thread 1–2in (2.5–5cm) up from where it emerges from the fabric. Wrap the thread around the needle one to three times then re-insert just the tip of the needle at 2, very close to 1, but not in the same hole. Use the hand holding the thread to pull gently so that the knot slips down around the needle and against the fabric. Maintain a gentle tension on the thread as you draw the needle through. This will help keep your thread from getting tangled.

Note: To make a larger knot, increase the number of strands of embroidery floss used and/or the number of times the thread is wrapped around the needle.

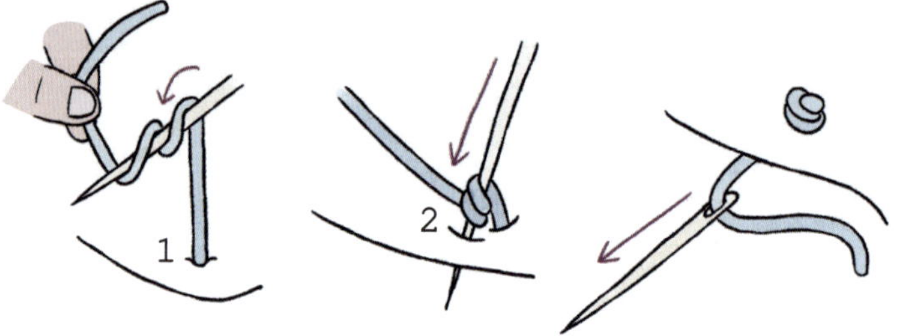

SATIN STITCH

A series of straight stitches used to fill in an area. Bring the needle up at 1 at the edge of the shape you're filling in. Reinsert at 2 at the opposite edge of the shape, creating a straight stitch. Continue making parallel straight stitches very close to one another as you fill in the shape.

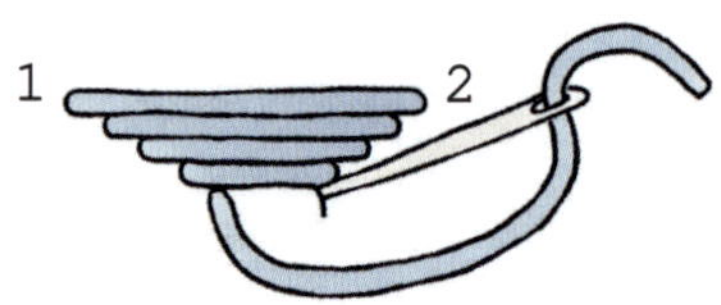

HOW TO SECURE YOUR EMBROIDERY THREAD

HOW TO SECURE THE BEGINNING OF YOUR EMBROIDERY THREAD

When you sew a doll using the sandwich method (like the projects in Section 1), it's easy to add detail to your doll with embroidery before sewing the pieces together. However, when you move to the construction methods used in Sections 2 and 3, embroidery detail is often added after the doll has been sewn and stuffed. This brings up the issue of how to hide the knots of your embroidery thread. There are several ways to do this. Each method requires a long doll needle. Try a few different methods until you find the one with which you feel most comfortable.

POP IT THROUGH

Make a smallish knot near the end of your thread. Insert the threaded doll needle on the back side of the head or a hidden area of your doll's face. Come out where you would like your first stitch. Gently tug the thread until it "pops" through the fabric. This seems frightening at first, but it works surprisingly well and does not leave a hole or mark on the fabric. This works less well if your fabric has a very tight weave or if you're using more than three strands of embroidery floss; the knot may be too large.

HIDE THE KNOT

This method is somewhat self-explanatory. Make a knot at the end of your thread and trim the ends very close to the knot. Begin your stitching in a hidden area such as underneath the arm where it will attach to the body (this is easier to do before the arm is sewn on), or behind or under an ear.

ANCHOR KNOT BEFORE STUFFING

This method requires forethought because the thread must be inserted before the doll is stuffed. Once the doll has been sewn and turned right side out, thread a doll needle with embroidery floss knotted at one end. Insert the needle through the opening which was left for turning and stuffing, emerging wherever you would like your first stitch to begin, for instance at the tip of the nose. Pull the knot into place and remove the needle. Admittedly, it can be a bit annoying to have the thread dangling as you stuff the doll, but I like that I can use a large, very secure knot.

HOW TO SECURE THE END OF YOUR EMBROIDERY THREAD

HIDE THE KNOT

Once you've completed your stitching, insert the doll needle so that it comes out in an area that is (or will be) hidden. I like to anchor knots on a seam if there's one handy because the multiple layers of fabric make the area stronger. Once you have tied your knot, reinsert the needle into the seam just next to the knot and emerge a short distance away. Pull the thread tightly so that the knot sinks down a bit into the seam and clip off close to the fabric so that the end of the thread disappears back into the doll.

DON'T KNOT

To be completely honest, this method makes me nervous, but it is quite a common practice with doll-makers, especially for dolls that will not be played with extensively. Complete your stitching then insert the doll needle so that it comes out as far away from the stitching as possible. Use the full extent of the long doll needle. Pull the thread through and clip it off close to the fabric so that the end of the thread disappears back into the doll. As long as the embroidery stitches are not pulled on or picked at by little fingers, you should be fine.

CHEEKS

Sweet pink cheeks bring life to a lovie. If your doll was made with light-colored fabric, you have several options. Always test first on a scrap of the same fabric you used to make your doll. Layer on color little by little, building up slowly until the cheeks have the desired shape and color. Take care not to rub too hard, as excess friction can cause the fabric to wear or fray. With these methods the color could fade over time and you may want to reapply in the future.

POWDER BLUSH

Be sure to use powder blush, not cream blush. Apply with a clean eye-shadow applicator or small craft or makeup brush. Load the applicator with blush, blow off the excess, and lightly brush onto your doll's cheeks.

BEESWAX CRAYON

Apply crayon to a clean piece of cotton fabric and use that as an applicator to gently rub onto your doll's cheeks. (See opposite.)

COLORED PENCIL

Using a good-quality colored pencil, gently draw in cheeks and blend with a clean piece of cotton fabric. Prismacolor Premier colored pencils and Faber-Castell Chalk Pencils are recommended.

For any doll, including those made with darker fabric, try one of the following options to add color to your doll's cheeks:

APPLIQUÉ

Add cheeks with felt appliqué just as we're using on Baby Bear's face and tummy (see page 46). You can either machine sew or hand appliqué felt cheeks onto your lovie. To appliqué fabric cheeks, jump forward to page 46 or page 60 for instructions on how to do so.

EMBROIDERY

Outline cheeks with backstitch then fill in with satin stitch (see page 30).

designing

DOLL-DESIGNING

Doll-designing is an art not a science. You begin with an idea, a spark of inspiration and a desire to create. If you pursue it, the creative process will lead you from point A (the idea) to point B (the doll). How you get there will be unique to you and to each idea. The process is very rarely a linear one, but rather a circuitous adventure involving a lot of experimentation and trial and error. As I have said many times already, there are no rules to follow and no road map. The best things you can do are to become familiar with as many techniques and construction methods as possible (giving you a larger knowledge base to draw from when designing), to be open to exploration and discovery, and to learn from the inevitable mistakes. The wonderful thing about doll-making is that even your "mistakes" can still be pretty cute.

TOOLS FOR DOLL-DESIGNING

You already have most of the tools you'll need on hand. In addition, there are a few tools that can be very useful and make the process easier for you.

- Pencil and a good eraser
- Tracing paper
- Regular or graph paper
- Flexible measuring tape
- Straight ruler
- ***French curve ruler*** (optional, but recommended) – It will help you draw smooth curved lines and make it much easier to add seam allowances to curved edges
- ***Seam gauge*** (optional) – This tool can also be used to add seam allowances, but if you have a French curve, you won't also need a seam gauge

DEVELOPING YOUR AESTHETIC

When you begin designing it makes sense to explore many styles, to experiment with different techniques and to emulate doll-makers that you admire. Journaling, mood boards and Pinterest can help you hone in on the aesthetic you aspire to. Gather images that inspire you and pay attention to what you're drawn to in others' work. Play, explore, make choices from a place of curiosity, and dabble in different styles to see which ones feel authentic to you. Over time, with practice and thoughtful experimentation, your work will begin to develop a visual language and aesthetic that is uniquely your own.

USING SOURCE MATERIALS

When designing animal dolls, we're not trying to replicate the image of an actual animal, but rather to create a character, tell a story or evoke a feeling. This gives us an enormous amount of freedom. Seeking out varied source materials can help us generate ideas and then pinpoint our direction.

Although realism is not our goal, photographs of animals are still our best resource. Look for photographs that show the animal from a range of angles and in different poses, close up and from far away. Illustrations from children's books are another favorite resource and can inspire us to think outside the box. Studying how stuffed animals are designed can be very interesting and give us insight into more complicated, three-dimensional construction methods. Finally, it can be enormously helpful to study other doll patterns to see how designers have tackled various technical and construction issues.

SKETCHING

Every new design starts with sketching, lots of sketching. Begin with simple shapes – circles, ovals, rectangles, triangles – to form the basic structure. The sketches do not need to be artistic or refined.

Experiment with different ideas, trying out various body and head shapes and playing around with different proportions. Once you have an overall shape that you're excited about, start adding in more detail, like placement of the eyes, angle of the ears, shape of the snout, etc. Working though an idea on paper is a lot easier than doing it with cloth so it pays to spend time with this phase of the design process.

Remember that realism is not the goal. Rather think stylized and exaggerated, more like a caricature of an animal. This is done by bringing out certain features while simplifying others. I think of this process as creating a character and a narrative, similar to what a children's book illustrator might do. We want the doll to convey emotion and personality. It is common with this style of doll for the head to be quite large in proportion to the body. Perhaps this is because the head is where the majority of character is conveyed or perhaps because it more closely mimics baby/toddler proportions which are so cute. However, there are no rules of proportion that need to be followed, so feel free to experiment.

Similarly, there is opportunity to add character by exaggerating the proportions of the body. Consider the length, shape and size of the torso in relation to the head, as well as the torso-to-limb ratio. A doll with very long arms and legs will give a different impression to one with short arms and legs. Another consideration when designing the body is what the doll will wear once completed. For a doll that will be fully clothed, I tend to make the torso narrower and the legs longer, whereas for a doll who will wear only a bandana or a bow tie, a round tummy and short little legs can be very sweet.

When designing dolls made with the sandwich method (like those in Section 1), it's important to consider how best to express the foreshortened features in two dimensions. When designing dolls with dimensionality like the ones in Sections 2 and 3, sketches need to include both front and side views. It requires a mental leap to visualize how a figure will look in three dimensions. Refer back to your source materials, if necessary, especially the photographs of animals.

TIPS FOR PATTERN-MAKING

- All designing should occur without using seam allowances.
- Keep in mind that when converting a two-dimensional pattern piece to a sewn and stuffed three-dimensional object, its size and shape will change in the process. The stuffed item will always be smaller and narrower than the flat paper pattern piece because of the way the fabric curves in toward the seams. Take this into account when drawing out pattern pieces.
- When designing a symmetrical pattern piece, design on a folded piece of paper and cut the pattern from the folded paper to ensure both sides match perfectly.
- When designing pattern pieces that will be sewn together, the length of their adjoining edges must be equal; the shapes of the pieces can be different, but the length of the seams must match. Accordingly, if you change one pattern piece, you may well need to adjust a corresponding piece.
- Staying organized will save you time and effort. Keep your desk/work area clean so you don't lose any of the little pieces.
- Document your work. This documentation will serve as a reference for future designs and help you replicate successful designs. This will be explained further in the prototyping section (see page 40).

ADAPTING A PATTERN

Using an existing pattern as a base to work from is a valid and efficient way to develop a new idea or personalize a design. There is no need to reinvent the wheel each time we design a doll. It's also a great way to learn and gain experience with pattern-making. To be clear, I am not condoning copying or passing someone else's design off as our own. The intention is to modify a pattern with the goal of creating something new and original. Eventually, with experience, we can use our own patterns as a starting-off point.

In Section 1, we'll look at a few methods for altering patterns – pattern slicing and lengthening or widening a pattern piece. You can try mixing and matching pieces from different patterns. This is easier with simple, separate elements, for instance ears or arms that are attached after the main piece has been sewn and stuffed. You can also use a photocopier to reduce or enlarge pattern pieces. Keep in mind that scaling by a large degree will change the proportions of the piece, especially any very wide or very narrow areas. And, remember that changing a pattern piece which will be sewn to a different pattern piece requires that you change the second piece accordingly so that they fit when sewn together.

PROTOTYPING

The next step is to test the newly designed or adapted pattern by sewing a prototype. A prototype is made with muslin or inexpensive fabric and without finishing details, allowing us to work through a design more quickly and to make changes or refinements. Just about every new design (or modification to an existing pattern) will need to be edited in some way before it is satisfactory, and you should expect to make several prototypes of each new design. Even experienced designers rarely get it right the first time out of the gate with a new design. This process is all about trial and error.

Each prototype should be completely and carefully stuffed in order to get a clear picture of its true size and shape. Muslin is a good choice for prototyping not only because it's inexpensive, but also because it's not very stretchy. Using stretchy fabric for a prototype would make it difficult to gauge its true shape.

Make minimal changes with each iteration. If we try changing too many things at once with each new prototype, it becomes impossible to decipher which changes had what effect. You will see that even small changes to the shape of a pattern can lead to remarkably different results.

When revising a pattern, do not cut or make alterations to the current pattern piece, as tempting and expedient as it may seem. Instead, trace or photocopy the current pattern piece (without seam allowance) onto a fresh piece of paper and make alterations to that. Documenting our work is an essential part of the prototyping process.

TIPS FOR DOCUMENTING PROTOTYPES

- Retain the pattern pieces for each version of your prototype: it's often necessary to return to a previous version or you may want to use a pattern piece for a different, future design.
- Label all pattern pieces with the name of the design, the name of the pattern piece and which version it is, i.e. Bunny Rabbit Head 3. Include all pertinent markings, such as dart markings or where to leave an opening for turning and stuffing.
- Label prototype dolls. Either attach a tag to the completed prototype which lists which version of each part was used, i.e. Head 2, Gusset 3, Body 3, etc. or, write the version number directly on each individual body part with a permanent marker pen.
- Take notes on your process. Do not assume that you will remember what you've done. Write down changes you've made or would like to make in future prototypes.

Once the design development process is complete, what is to be done with all the prototypes? You may choose to keep a few lying around the studio as reference or for sentimental reasons; in time they might inspire new designs. Giving them away is one option, especially if you have young ones in your life who are perhaps not too judgmental about slightly funny-looking dolls. Another option is to recycle the stuffing and salvage as much of the fabric as possible to be used for future prototyping, especially for smaller pieces like ears and arms.

NOTE

As designers, we have the opportunity to use the design process as a means to draw out and emphasize the aspects of doll-making that we enjoy most and do what we can to minimize the parts we don't like as much. For instance, stuffing is my least favorite step, so over time my dolls have gotten smaller and smaller. (Hello little Mouse!)

Similarly, I'm always interested in finding the simplest, sparest way to design a doll with the least number of steps and elements. I love nothing more, aesthetically-speaking, than the elegance of simplicity. Perhaps you, on the other hand, are a maximalist who will want to cover your dolls with embroidery and design details or an engineer who will choose to tackle elaborate and complicated design problems. You do you!

Above all, I hope that with curiosity and continued exploration, you will discover ways to express your authentic and unique point of view while finding as much fun and delight as possible in the process of designing and making dolls.

SECTION ONE

All the projects in Section 1 are made with a simple construction method which I call the "sandwich method". At its most basic, "sandwich method" construction consists of two pieces of fabric, a front and back which are sewn with right sides together, turned right side out and stuffed. The pattern we'll be using incorporates the head, torso and legs in one pattern piece, while appendages like arms, wings or ears are sandwiched between the front and back pieces and sewn directly into the seam. With the first few projects we'll be using essentially the same basic pattern and focusing on various techniques for embellishing our dolls. Then we'll learn how to alter and add complexity to the basic pattern.

baby bear

Made with a simple pattern and a very basic "sandwich method" construction, we'll use felt appliqué to bring life and character to our Baby Bear doll. You'll see how just a few details can add so much sweetness and personality.

SKILL LEVEL: BEGINNER

FINISHED SIZE: 10IN (25.5CM)

MATERIALS AND SPECIAL TOOLS FOR BABY BEAR

- Pattern pieces (see pages 15 and 79)
- **Fabric A**, medium-weight cotton or linen/cotton blend: 18 x 12in (46 x 30.5cm)
  - Body x 2: Cut 1 pair
  - Ear x 4: Sew 2 pairs
  - Arm x 4: Sew 2 mirrored pairs
- **Felt A**, color of your choice: 4 x 3in (10 x 7.5cm)
  - Snout x 1
  - Tummy x 1
- **Felt B**, white: 1½ x 1in (4 x 2.5cm) scrap
  - Eye x 2: ½in (1.2cm) circles
- **Felt C**, black: 1¼ x 1¼in (3 x 3cm) scrap
  - Pupil x 2: ¼in (6mm) circles
  - Nose x 1
- Embroidery floss (thread) in black
- Freezer paper (optional)
- ¼in (6mm) hole punch (optional)
- Powder blush, beeswax crayon, colored pencil, or pink felt for cheeks (optional)

FELT APPLIQUÉ

Appliqué is an easy and versatile technique for adding detail to a design. The process involves attaching a smaller piece of fabric to a larger piece of fabric in order to make a design. Felt is an ideal fabric for this because its edges don't fray when cut. You can appliqué by hand with whipstitch (see page 30) or with your sewing machine.

MACHINE APPLIQUÉ

1. To begin, position the felt piece on the background fabric and pin to hold in place.
2. Use your machine's regular straight stitch with a 2.5mm stitch length for larger felt pieces or a shorter stitch length of 2mm for very small pieces. Sew all the way around the felt piece ⅛in (3mm) or less from the edge, maintaining an even distance from the edge and a smooth line. Do not backstitch to secure stitches at the beginning of the seam. Instead, once you've come all the way around, continue to sew over the beginning stitches then backstitch to secure the seam.
3. For very small felt pieces, you may need to pivot the fabric around after every stitch or two so that the stitches remain right on the edge of the felt. Set your machine to leave the needle in the down position after each stitch. If your machine doesn't have that setting, manually lower the needle back through the fabric after each stitch to hold it in place as you lift the foot and pivot the fabric.

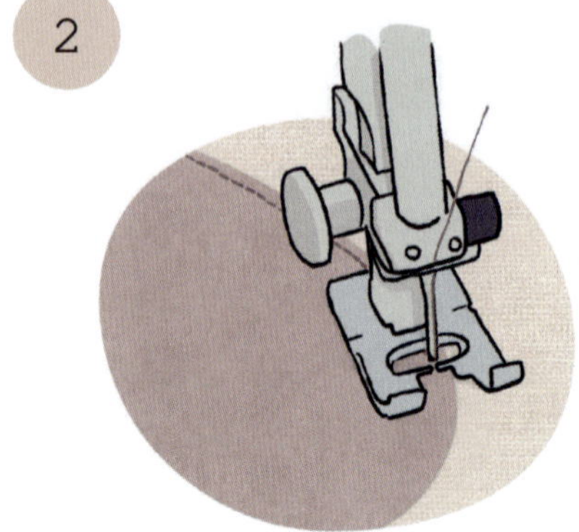

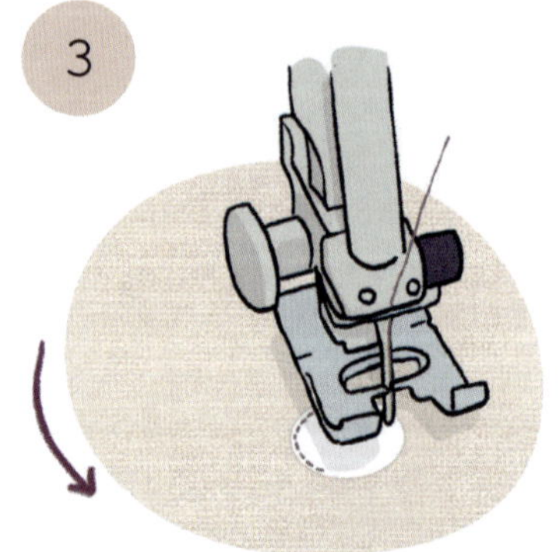

FREEZER PAPER

Despite its many wonderful qualities, a challenge with felt is that its fuzzy texture makes it difficult to trace onto when transferring a pattern. I recommend using freezer paper to transfer a pattern to felt. Freezer paper is a thick white paper with wax or plastic on one side. You can easily trace your pattern onto the matte paper side and iron it onto wool felt (see note) with the waxy, shiny side face down on the felt. The heat of the iron will melt the wax and temporarily bond it to the felt. Later, the paper peels off easily without leaving any residue.

NOTE:

Do not iron synthetic felt. It may melt. It's okay to use a cool iron with wool-blend felt.

Once you have traced the pattern onto freezer paper, there are two options:

OPTION 1

Either cut the pattern out of freezer paper first before ironing it to the felt, then carefully cut the felt around the freezer paper.

OPTION 2

Or, leave a border around the pattern so that once you've ironed it to the felt, you can cut through the freezer paper and felt at the same time, following the lines to get a lovely, clean edge (see the photograph above left).

The second method may give you more accurate results, but one of the benefits of using freezer paper is that you can reuse the pattern piece many times. If your pattern calls for multiples of a pattern piece, for instance two eyes or two cheeks, it may make more sense to use the first method so that your pattern piece can be reused.

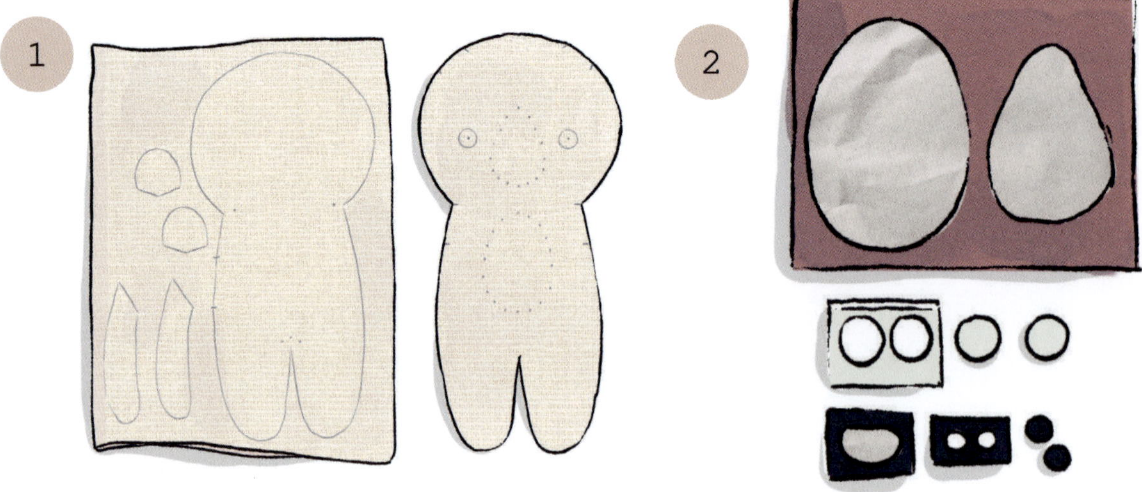

1. *Transfer patterns and markings for all pieces as follows*. Take care to transfer the correct lines as indicated: either the stitch line (without seam allowance) or the cutting line (with seam allowance included). When transferring stitch lines, be sure to leave ample space around the pattern pieces.

   On the 18 x 12in (46 x 30.5cm) piece of **Fabric A** which has been folded in half with right sides together so that you will have mirrored pieces, transfer the Body pattern on the cutting line. Once cut, transfer face detail, Tummy, Ear and Arm placement markings to the right side of the Front piece and transfer neck, crotch and opening marks to the wrong side of the Back piece. The right-side markings are used to help position added elements (Arms, Ears, appliqué), while the wrong-side markings on the Back piece show us exactly where to begin and end our seam line and where to pivot (at neck and crotch) when sewing to get a clean and even shape.

   On the same folded piece of **Fabric A**, transfer Arm and Ear patterns twice each on the stitch line.

   On **Felt A, B, C** transfer all the pieces on the cutting line (see illustration 2).

2. Cut out all pieces for which you transferred cutting lines. Cut out felt pieces using freezer paper (see page 47). For the tiniest piece, try using a ¼in (6mm) hole punch.

CONTINUES...

3. ***Arms*** – Sew the Arms directly on the stitch line, leaving the top edge open. Cut out around the sewing lines with pinking shears. Turn right side out and press out the seams. Stuff the Arms to about ½in (1.2cm) below the opening.

4. ***Ears*** – Sew the Ears together in pairs, along the stitch line, leaving the bottom edge open. Cut out around the sewing lines with pinking shears. Turn right side out and press out seams. Fold each Ear in half. Starting at the bottom of the Ear, sew ½in (1.2cm) up along the fold, 3⁄16 in (5mm) from the edge. Repeat for the second Ear.

5. ***Appliqué*** – Position felt pieces using the markings, then pin in place. Appliqué by hand with whipstitch (see page 30) or by machine (see page 46).

- For the Snout and Tummy, use a stitch length of 2.5mm.

- For (white) Eye pieces, use a shorter stitch length of 2mm and pivot the fabric around after every stitch or two. Try to maintain an even distance from the edge and a smooth line because this stitch line will be visible and will affect your bear's expression.

- Layer the Nose piece over the Snout. Again, use a stitch length of 2mm and pivot the fabric as necessary.

- For (black) Pupil pieces, take care to choose a position that you like as this will determine whether your Bear has a naughty, worried or playful look. Be sure that the Pupils are at an even height and equidistant from the edges of the white portion of the eye. Hand sew the Pupil pieces over the Eye pieces with strong black thread, making two straight stitches in an X shape. Stitch over the X several times to secure it well.

6. ***Embroider mouth*** – Using 3 strands of black embroidery floss, bring the needle out from under the center bottom of the nose at 1. Come straight down to insert at 2. Emerge at 3. Bring the needle under the stitch between 1 and 2 and re-insert at 4.

7. ***Baste Ears to Front piece*** – Using markings, position the Ears on the Front piece with right sides together. Align the inner corner of each Ear with the edge of the Front piece. The outer corner angles out to overlap the Front piece by ¼in (6mm). Baste in place ⅛in (3mm) from the edge.

8. ***Baste Arms to Front piece*** – Using markings, position the Arms on the right side of the Front piece, aligning raw edges. Baste in place ⅛in (3mm) in from the edge.

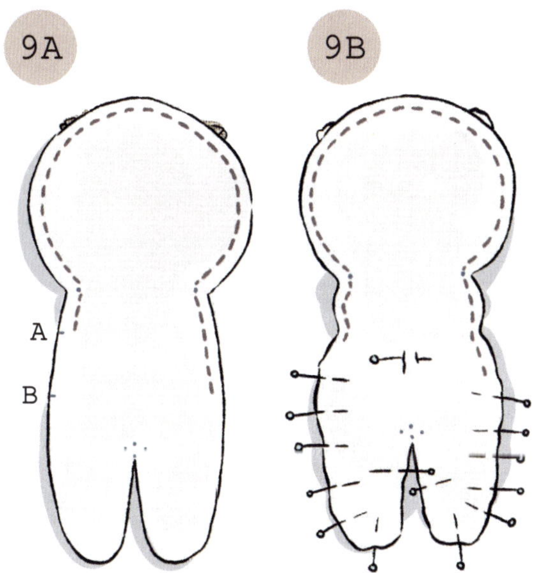

9. ***Sew Body*** – Lay the Back piece over the Front piece with right sides together and pin to secure. If the Arms get in the way of pinning the crotch area neatly, leave that area unpinned for now. Begin sewing at A. Sew around, pausing at neck markings with the needle in the down position in order to pivot the fabric. Once you have sewn around the head and down the other side, backstitch to secure the seam (see illustration 9A). Take your work off the machine so that you can tuck the arms farther up into the doll. Pin the fabric just below the arms to hold them out of the way. Pin around crotch and legs, being careful that the fabric lays flat and that the layers are lined up correctly (see illustration 9B).

10. Continue sewing, pausing at crotch markings to pivot the fabric. If necessary, readjust the arms and re-pin when coming around to the other side of the crotch. Finish sewing to B, leaving the opening as marked. Reinforce seams at neck/arm and crotch with an extra line of stitching. Clip corners/curves and trim the seam allowance with pinking shears (see page 22). Turn right side out and press out the seams.

11. ***Stuff and close*** – Stuff the body until packed firmly then close with ladder stitch.

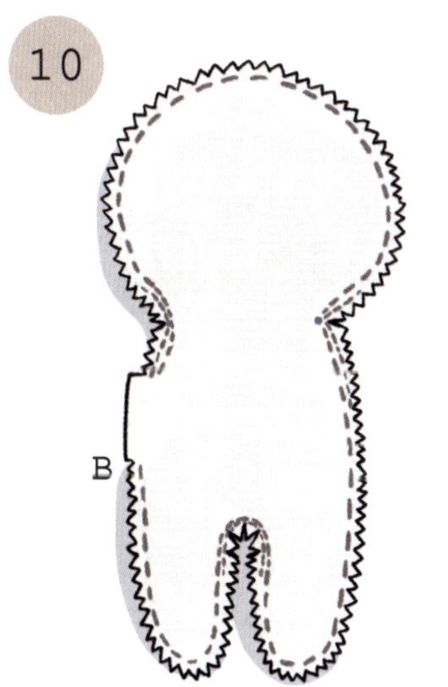

This project uses the same body pattern as the Baby Bear, swapping out the ears and exchanging arms for wings to create our sweet and wise little Owl friend. This project will give us an opportunity to explore embroidery as an embellishment technique, practicing several simple and very useful stitches to create the Owl's face, glasses and feathers.

SKILL LEVEL: BEGINNER

FINISHED SIZE: 10IN (25.5CM)

MATERIALS AND SPECIAL TOOLS FOR OWL

- Pattern pieces (see the inside-front cover and page 15)
- **Fabric A**, medium-weight cotton or linen/cotton blend: 18 x 12in (46 x 30.5cm)
  - Body x 2: Cut 1 pair
  - Ear x 4: Sew 2 pairs
  - Wing x 2: Sew 2 mirrored pairs from **Fabric A** and **B**
- **Fabric B**, medium-weight cotton or linen/cotton blend: 6½ x 4½in (16.5 x 11.5cm)
  - Wing x 2: Sew 2 mirrored pairs from **Fabric A** and **B**
- Iron-on interfacing: 6 x 8in (15.5 x 20.5cm) (optional)
- Embroidery floss in black and the color(s) of your choice
- 5in (12.5cm) embroidery hoop (optional)
- Powder blush, beeswax crayon, colored pencil or pink felt for cheeks (optional)

PATTERN NOTE

I recommend using iron-on interfacing if you are using a light-colored fabric where the embroidery floss on the back may show through. It will also add stability to your fabric and help prevent any puckering around the embroidery.

SEWING INSTRUCTIONS FOR OWL

1. *Prepare fabric and transfer patterns* – Take care to transfer the correct lines as indicated: either the stitch line (without seam allowance) or the cutting line (with seam allowance included). When transferring stitch lines, be sure to leave ample space around the pattern pieces for the seam allowance.

   A) Fold a 12 x 13½in (30.5 x 34.5cm) piece of **Fabric A** in half with right sides together to 6 x 13½in (15.25 x 34.5cm). The fold should run parallel to the selvedge edge.

   B) If you are using the optional iron-on interfacing, lay it over the folded fabric, aligning the top edges so that a strip of fabric at the bottom remains uncovered. Bond using the product's directions. Keeping the fabric folded, flip it over so that the patterns are transferred to the other side without interfacing.

   C) Transfer Body pattern on cutting line to the top portion of the folded fabric. Transfer neck, crotch and opening markings. This will be the Back Body piece. All other markings will be transferred to the Front Body after the pieces have been cut out. If using interfacing, the side with the interfacing is the Front Body piece.

   D) On the same piece of fabric, transfer the Ear pattern twice on the stitch line to the bottom portion of the fabric (without interfacing).

   E) Cut 6½ x 4½in (16.5 x 11.5cm) piece each of **Fabrics A** and **B**. Lay one over the other with right sides together and transfer Wing pattern twice on stitch line. Remember to flip over the pattern piece after the first wing, in order to have a mirrored set.

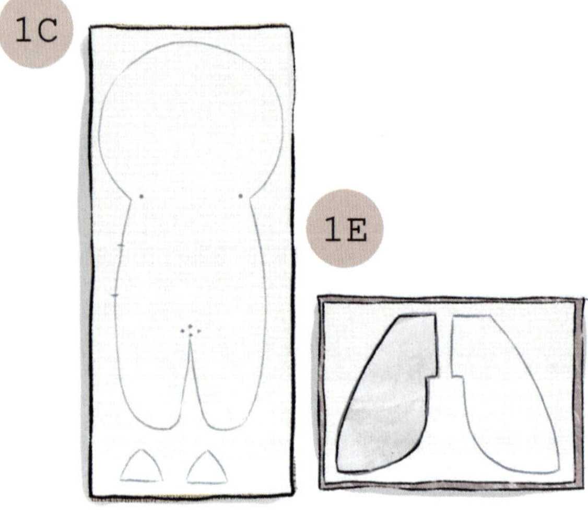

2. *Cut out Body pieces* along the cutting lines.

3. *Sew Ears* directly on the stitch line. Note that the bottom edge is a cutting line and is left open for turning. Cut out around the sewing line with pinking shears. Turn right side out and press out seams. Fold over as indicated on the pattern, making sure that the two Ears mirror each other. Baste by hand or machine along the bottom edge to hold the fold in place.

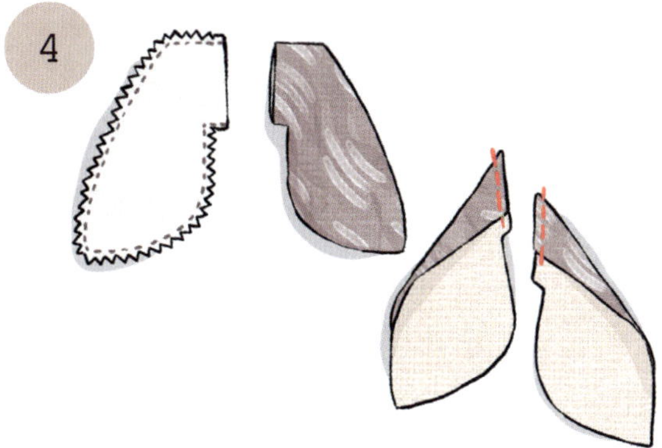

4. *Sew Wings* directly on the stitch line, leaving openings as marked. Cut out around the sewing line with pinking shears (see page 22). Turn right side out and press out seams. With **Fabric A** on the inside and **Fabric B** on the outside, fold over the top edge of each wing so that it lines up with the opening edge. Make sure that the two pieces mirror each other. Baste by hand or machine along opening edge to hold the fold in place.

5. Transfer the following markings to the right side of the Front Body piece: neck, ear and wing placement markings, and face and feather details.

6. ***Embroider face and feathers*** **–** Use three strands of black embroidery floss for eyes, eyebrow dots, nose and mouth. Use three strands of embroidery floss in the color(s) of your choice for glasses and feathers. See Embroidery Stitches on pages 29–30, and use an embroidery hoop if it helps.

- Use running stitch for the glasses
- Use backstitch to ring the eyes and satin stitch to fill them in
- Use a French knot for each eyebrow dot
- Use backstitch to ring the nose and satin stitch to fill it in
- Use a straight stitch for the mouth. Add a tacking stitch to make it curve
- Use fly stitch for the feathers

CONTINUES...

7. ***Baste Ears and Wings to Front Body piece***. Using markings, position the Ears on the Front Body piece with right sides together, aligning the raw edges. Note that the narrower of the folded sides is face down while the folded edge faces towards the center of the head. Baste in place ⅛in (3mm) from the edge. Using markings, position the Wings on the Front Body piece with right sides together, aligning raw edges. Note that **Fabric A** is face down. Baste in place ⅛in (3mm) from the edge.

8. Once basted, carefully ***fold the wings*** away from the sides so that they will not get sewn into the seams. Use either a tacking stitch or a pin to hold them in place. If using a pin, be sure to angle the head of the pin towards the opening so that later you will be able to pull it out through the opening before turning the piece right side out.

9. ***Sew Body.*** Lay the Back Body piece over the Front Body piece with right sides facing. Sew around from A to B, pausing at neck and crotch markings with the needle in the down position in order to pivot the fabric. Leave the opening for turning and stuffing. Reinforce seams at neck/wing and crotch. Clip curves/corners and trim seam allowance with pinking shears (see page 22). Remove the pin holding the wings in place. Turn right side out and press out seams.

10. ***Stuff the Body*** until packed firmly, then close with ladder stitch.

kitty

For our Kitty doll, we'll alter the simple pattern we've been using by changing some pattern pieces and adding others. You'll see how easy it can be to take an existing pattern and make it your own. We'll also add fabric appliqué to our toolbox of embellishment techniques.

SKILL LEVEL: CONFIDENT BEGINNER

FINISHED SIZE: 11½IN (29CM)

MATERIALS AND SPECIAL TOOLS FOR KITTY

- Pattern pieces (see the inside-front cover and pages 15 and 77)
- **Fabric A**, medium-weight cotton or linen/cotton blend: 12 x 10½in (30.5 x 27cm)
    - – Head x 2: Cut 1 pair
    - – Foot x 4: Cut 2 mirrored pairs
    - – Arm x 4: Sew 2 mirrored pairs
- **Fabric B**, medium-weight cotton or linen/cotton blend: 13 x 9in (33 x 23cm)
    - – Body x 2: Cut 1 pair
    - – Ear x 4: Cut 2 pairs
    - – Muzzle x 1: Cut 1
- **Felt** (black): 1 x 2in (2.5 x 5cm)
    - – Eyes x 2
    - – Nose x 1
- Woven iron-on interfacing (optional): 6 x 5in (15 x 13cm)
    - – Interfacing x 1 (see page 77)
- Embroidery floss in white, black and pink
- Freezer paper (optional)
- Doll needle and strong thread to attach arms
- Powder blush, beeswax crayon, colored pencil, or pink felt for cheeks (optional)

FABRIC APPLIQUÉ

In this project we'll appliqué fabric as opposed to felt which we used previously. The process is a bit different because fabric has raw edges so we'll use the zig-zag stitch on our sewing machine to secure the raw edges and keep them from fraying.

When choosing fabric for this project, it's important to take into account its stretchiness. Try to choose fabrics with a relatively tight weave and less stretch. Consider that when we stuff a doll it causes the fabric to stretch and strains the appliqué stitching. If the fabric is very stretchy while the appliqué stitching remains tight, your Kitty may look misshapen or worse yet, the stitching could tear the appliqué fabric as the background fabric stretches beneath it.

Woven iron-on interfacing can be used on the wrong side of the background fabric (in this pattern the Head) to help keep it from stretching as much. I recommend using interfacing if:

- You are using fabrics with a considerable amount of stretch
- The background fabric is stretchier than the appliqué fabric
- You tend to stuff dolls very tightly

An additional benefit of using iron-on interfacing is that it will help prevent your fabric from puckering when sewing with zig-zag stitch.

HOW TO MACHINE APPLIQUÉ WITH ZIG-ZAG STITCH

1. Position the appliqué piece using the markings on the pattern and pin to hold in place.
2. Set your machine to zig-zag stitch and adjust the stitch width and length. I recommend testing a few combinations of different widths and lengths on scrap fabric to find a look that you like. A very closely spaced zig-zag stitch using a shorter stitch length will give the look of an almost solid, thick line of stitching similar to satin stitch. The benefit of a closely spaced stitch is that it will contain the edges well and minimize fraying. On the other hand, the fabric is more likely to pucker. I use a width of 3mm and a length of 1.5mm. The edge of the appliqué fabric does fray a bit over time but I like the look of it.
3. Position the fabric on the machine so that the left leg of the zig-zag stitch goes into the appliqué fabric while the right leg of the stitch goes into the background fabric, just barely past the edge of the appliqué fabric. Sew around the appliqué piece. If necessary, pause with the needle down, lift the foot and reposition the fabric to pivot around curved areas. Backstitch to secure.

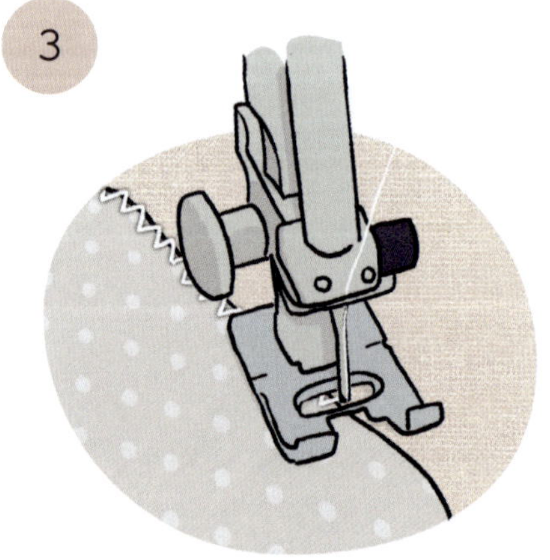

MODIFYING A PATTERN

PATTERN SLICING

One of the easiest ways to modify a pattern is with the addition of contrasting color or pattern. For the Kitty, we'll modify the pattern we've used in the last two projects which incorporates head, body and legs, by cutting it so that we have three separate pattern pieces – head, body and feet. This will give us the opportunity to add contrasting fabric.

- To do this, it's as simple as slicing the pattern, retracing the now separate pieces and adding a ¼in (6mm) seam allowance to each cut side. In this example, both slices are horizontal, but a slice can also be vertical or even diagonal. However, in every case, it is essential that the seam allowance be a perfect rectangle with all angles equal to 90 degrees. This will ensure we maintain the original shape of the outline when sewing the two pieces together.

PATTERN SLICING

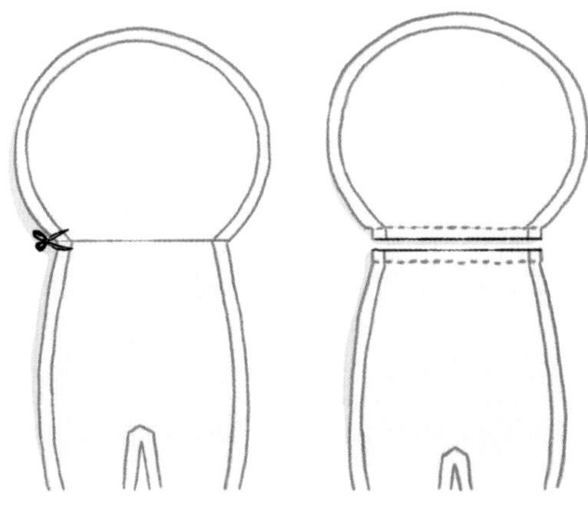

LENGTHEN OR WIDEN A PATTERN

Another easy way to alter a pattern is to lengthen or widen it. For the Kitty doll, we'll extend the legs of our original pattern. If the pattern piece being extended is rectangular, it's easy enough to add to the top, bottom or sides of the piece. However, most pattern pieces curve or taper, making things a bit more involved. In this case, the legs taper, as they go down, so adding length at the bottom would make them too narrow and pointy. Instead, the extra length is added to the interior of the pattern piece so that it maintains its general shape.

1. Remember when modifying a pattern to make changes to the sewing line, not the cutting line. If the pattern piece to be altered is symmetrical, begin by folding the pattern piece in half vertically and tracing or photocopying it onto a new sheet of paper. This way, modifications are made to one side only, ensuring the new pattern is also symmetrical.

2. Draw a horizontal line through the area to be lengthened. This is where we will cut and separate the pattern. In this example, the cut line is across the widest part of the leg, but we could add length anywhere along the pattern, like the torso or head. Draw a vertical line that bisects the horizontal line. This will help us correctly realign the halves after we've added length. Cut through the horizontal line, slicing the leg in two.

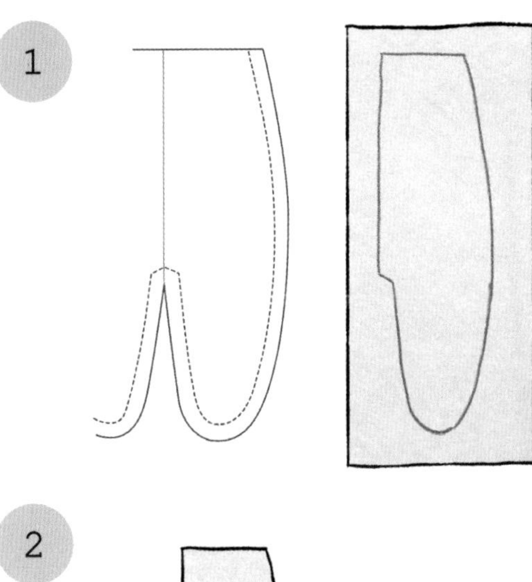

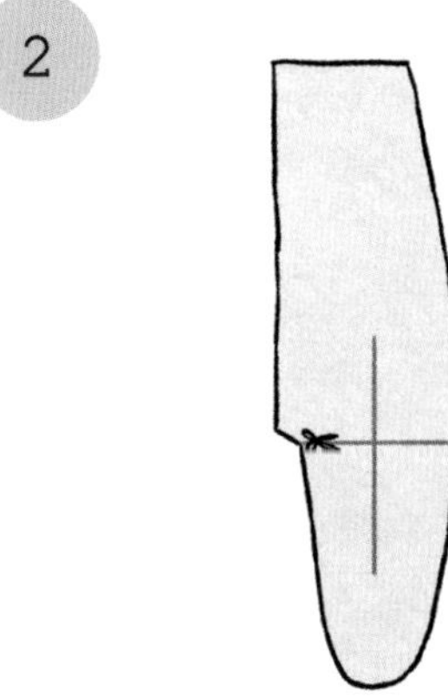

3. Cut a piece of paper to about 2in (5cm) wider than your pattern and at least 2in (5cm) longer than the added length. I chose to extend the Kitty legs by 1¼in (3cm). Place the piece of paper behind the upper pattern piece about 1in (2.5cm) above the cut line. Tape them together on the back. Draw a parallel line 1¼in (3cm) (or the amount of added length) below the cut line. Extend the vertical line from the upper pattern piece to meet the horizontal line you just drew. Tape the lower pattern piece to the paper using the vertical and horizontal lines as guides for placement.

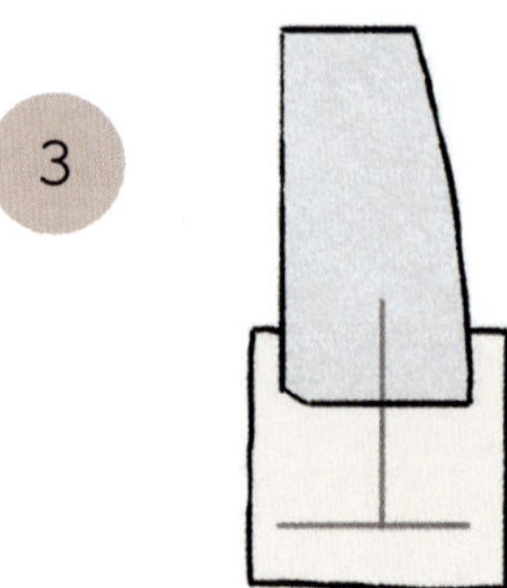

4. Using a ruler or French curve, if necessary, draw in the new sides to connect the upper and lower pieces. You may need to readjust things a bit to make a balanced shape. In this case, I shifted the bottom piece over to the right in order to maintain the same angle on the inside of the leg as in the original pattern.

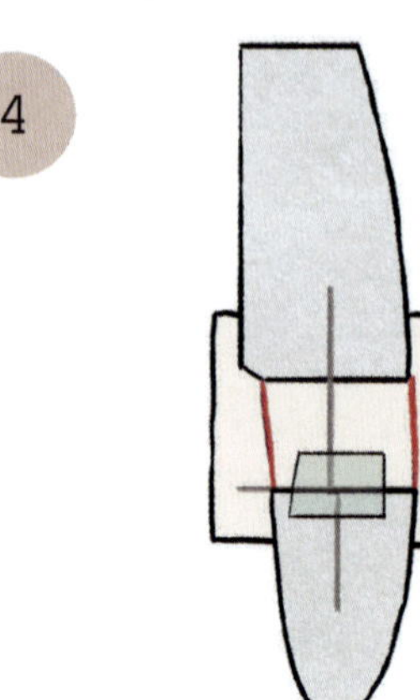

5. Trim excess paper. Place the modified pattern on a fresh sheet of folded paper, lining them up carefully along the folded edge. Trace the pattern, add in the seam allowance, then cut the new pattern from the folded paper.

To widen a pattern – follow the same directions, swapping the words "horizontal" and "vertical". For non-symmetrical pattern pieces, the directions are also the same but there will be no need to fold the piece in half.

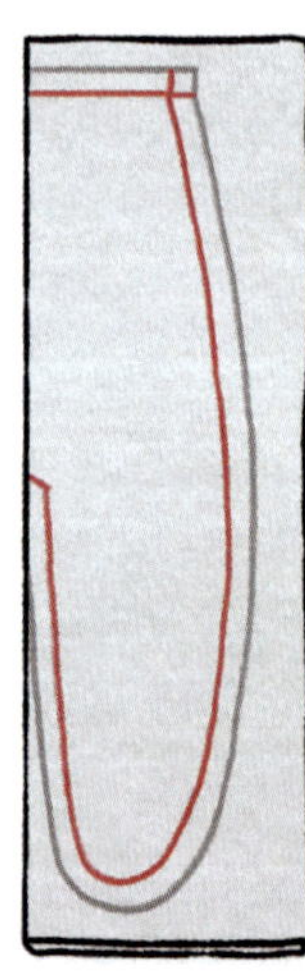

2–4

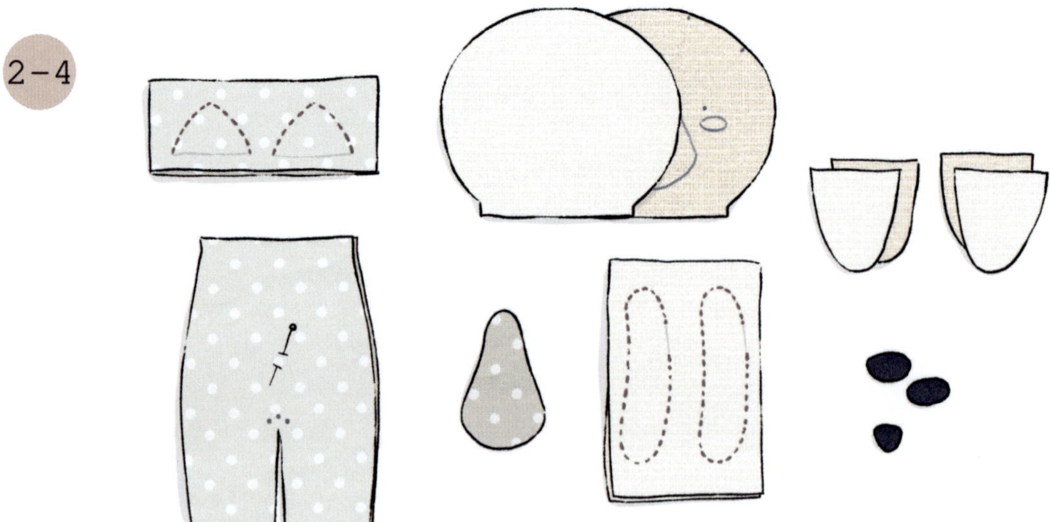

1. ***Transfer patterns and markings for all pieces as follows.*** Take note of which fabric you'll be using for each piece (**A** or **B**) and take care to transfer the correct lines as indicated: either the stitch line (without seam allowance) or the cutting line (with seam allowance included). When transferring stitch lines, be sure to leave ample space around the pattern pieces for seam allowance.

On the 12 x 10½in (30.5 x 27cm) piece of **Fabric A** which has been folded in half with right sides together so that you will have mirrored pieces, transfer the Head pattern on the cutting line. Once cut, transfer the face detail markings to right side of fabric (Head Front). Transfer the Foot pattern twice on the cutting line. Transfer the Arm pattern twice on the stitch line. Transfer markings for opening placement to wrong side of fabric.

On a 10½ x 9in (27 x 23cm) piece of **Fabric B** which has been folded in half with right sides together so that you will have mirrored pieces, transfer the Body pattern on the cutting line. Transfer markings for opening placement and crotch to wrong side of fabric (Body Back). Transfer the Ear pattern twice on the stitch line. Ears remain open at the bottom for turning.

On a 2½ x 3¾in (6.5 x 9.5cm) piece of **Fabric B**, transfer the Snout pattern on the cutting line.

On the woven iron-on interfacing (optional), transfer the Interfacing pattern on the cutting line.

On the **Felt**, transfer the Eye twice on the cutting line and the Nose once on the cutting line.

2. Cut out all pieces for which you transferred cutting lines.

3. *Add interfacing (if using)* – Lay the interfacing over the wrong side of the Head Front piece and bond using the product's directions. There's no need for interfacing on the back Head piece since we will not be appliquéing on that piece.

4 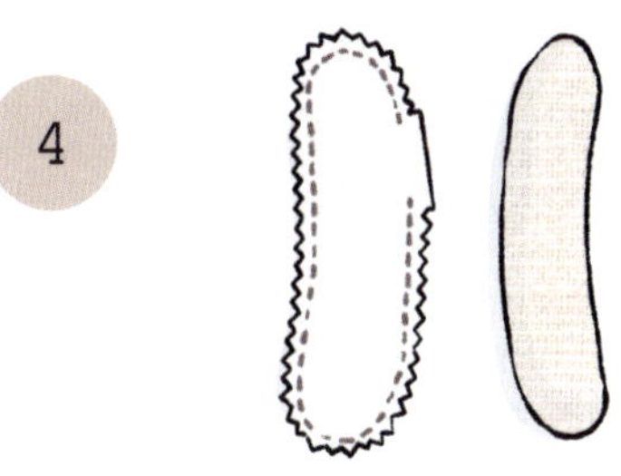

5 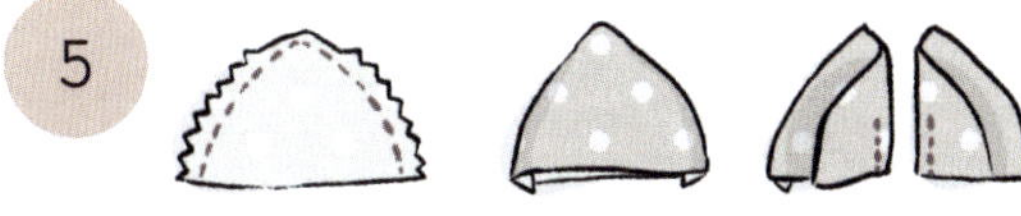

6 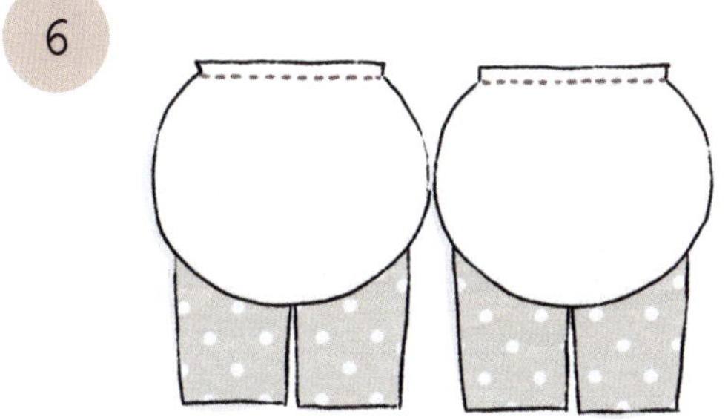

7 

9 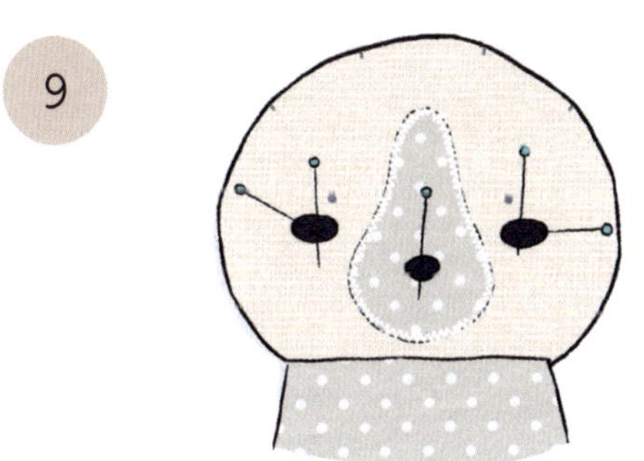

4. Sew all pieces for which you transferred stitch lines: Arms and Ears. Sew directly on the stitch line, leaving openings as marked. Cut out around the sewing line with pinking shears. Turn right side out and press out seams.

5. ***Prepare Ears*** – Fold Ears as indicated on the pattern. Starting at the bottom of the Ear, sew ½in (1.2mm) up along the fold ⅛in (3mm) from the edge. Repeat for the second Ear, making sure to fold in the other direction so that the ears are mirrored. Unfold Ears and press open.

6. ***Attach Head*** – Lay each Head piece over a Body piece with right sides together. Sew Head to Body. Press open seams. These are now called Body pieces.

7. ***Attach Foot pieces*** – Lay the Foot pieces over the Body pieces with right sides together, making sure the toes point towards the center. Sew Feet to Body. Press open seams.

8. ***Add Muzzle*** – Using markings to position, pin the Muzzle to the Body Front piece. Appliqué following the instructions on page 60.

9. Using markings to position, pin Eye and Nose pieces on the Head piece. Appliqué pieces by hand or machine. See instructions for whipstitch on page 30 or Felt Appliqué on page 46.

CONTINUES...

10. *Embroider face details* – see Embroidery Stitches on pages 29–30. With white embroidery floss, use vertical satin stitch to create the white part of the eyes and French knots to create the highlights in the eyes. With black embroidery floss, use straight stitch to embroider the mouth (see illustration 6 on page 50). Use Fench knots to create the eyebrow dots. If you are using light-colored fabric, trim the tails of the knots very short so that they don't show through the fabric. With pink embroidery floss, use French knots to create whisker dots on either side of the muzzle.

11. *Attach Ears* – Using markings, position the Ears on the Head piece with right sides together and the shorter folded sides of the Ears closer to the center. Let the outer corners of the Ears overlap the fabric so that the inner corners and center of the Ear match up with the raw edge of the Head piece. Pin or baste in place ⅛in (3mm) in from edge of the Head piece.

12. *Sew Body* – Lay the Back Body piece over the Front Body piece and pin together. Sew around, pausing at crotch markings with the needle in the down position in order to pivot the fabric. Leave opening for turning and stuffing. Reinforce seams at neck and crotch with an extra row of stitching. Clip curves/corners and trim seam allowance with pinking shears (see page 22). Turn right side out and press out seams.

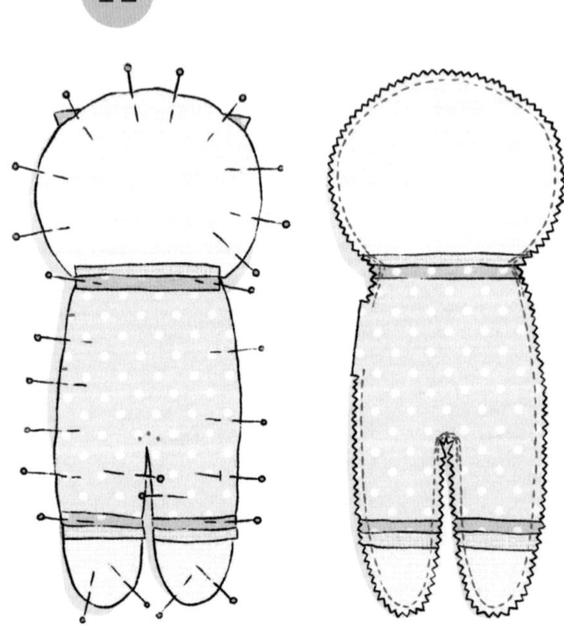

13. Stuff the Body and Arms until packed firmly then close with ladder stitch (see page 25).

14. *Attach Arms* – Position the Arms and attach to the Body (see pages 26–27). Be sure to face the ladder-stitched openings on the Arms toward the back.

monkey

Our monkey showcases the embellishment techniques we've used in the last few projects and takes our pattern alterations to a new level. The design features faux shorts created with the pattern-slicing technique we used in the last project, separate legs, which are sewn into the bottom seam, and some fun details like elbows, knees and a curvy tail. I hope this monkey gives you a sense of how detailed and dynamic a "sandwich method" doll can be.

SKILL LEVEL: ADVANCED

FINISHED SIZE: 14IN (36CM)

MATERIALS AND SPECIAL TOOLS FOR MONKEY

- Pattern pieces (see pages 15 and 77–78)
- **Fabric A**, medium-weight cotton or linen/cotton blend: 24½ x 6in (62 x 15cm)
  - – Head x 1: Cut 1
  - – Upper Body x 2: Cut 1 pair
  - – Arm x 4: Sew 2 mirrored pairs
  - – Ear x 4: Sew 2 pairs
- **Fabric B**, medium-weight cotton or linen/cotton blend: 6 x 13in (49.5 x 8cm)
  - – Head x 1: Cut 1
  - – Forehead x 1: Cut 1
  - – Tail x 2: Sew 1 mirrored pair
- **Fabric C**, medium-weight cotton or linen/cotton blend: 19½ x 3¼in (15 x 33cm)
  - – Lower Body x 2: Cut 1 pair
- **Fabric D**, medium-weight cotton or linen/cotton blend: 2½ x 3in (6.5 x 7.5cm)
  - – Tummy x 1: Cut 1
- **Fabric A/C**
  - – Leg x 4: Sew 2 mirrored pairs
- **Felt A**, color of your choice: 2¾ x1¾in (7 x 4.5cm)
  - – Snout x 1
- **Felt B** (white): 1½ x 1in (4 x 2.5cm) scrap
  - – Eye x 2: ½in (1.2cm) circles
- Woven iron-on interfacing (optional): 5¾ x 4¾in (14.5 x 12cm)
  - – Interfacing x 1
- Embroidery floss in black
- Doll eyes, 9mm
- Awl, ⅛in (3mm) hole punch or small scissors
- Freezer paper for cutting felt pieces (optional)
- Doll needle and strong thread to attach arms
- Powder blush, beeswax crayon, colored pencil, or pink felt for cheeks (optional)

ELBOWS AND KNEES

A very simple and cute way to give a bit of articulation to our monkey's arms and legs, is to add "elbows" and "knees." After the Arms and Legs have been sewn, turned right side out and pressed, but before they are stuffed, we will simply sew a few stitches either by hand or by machine.

1. Starting from the edge of the piece, sew in towards the center about ⅛–¼in (3–6mm) where marked on the pattern piece. Sew back and forth a few times to secure well. The knees have stitches on both the inner and outer sides of the Leg (see the photograph above left), while the elbow is stitched only on the back side of the Arm. Make sure that you leave a large enough gap between the lines of stitching on the Legs at the knees to enable you to stuff the lower section.

2. When stuffing the Arms and Legs, the more loosely you stuff in the area around the stitching, the more you will be able to bend the limbs.

ADDING A TAIL WITH THE SLIT METHOD

Our Monkey doll is one of only two dolls in this book with a tail. Knowing how wild monkeys can be, we'd best attach this tail very securely. A machine-sewn attachment, like sewing an arm or leg into a seam, is generally much stronger than a hand-sewn one. With the slit method we will create a seam, allowing us to attach the tail securely. This method can be used anytime you'd like to add pieces to your doll where there isn't a seam positioned where you need it.

1. Cut a slit where indicated on the pattern piece. You want the slit to be just long enough for the Tail to fit but no longer.
2. Insert the unstuffed Tail into the slit from the right side until it emerges about ⅛–¼in (3–6mm) on the wrong side. Fold the Lower Body piece in half with right sides together so that the slit edges are lined up evenly. Pin the Tail in place.
3. Machine sew the slit closed. Sew in a smooth arc shape from the folded edge, just before the start of the slit, arcing out to about ⅛in (3mm) in from the slit and then back to the folded edge on the other side of the slit. Check the back side to ensure that the stitching has caught all layers of fabric.
4. For extra reinforcement, run another line of stitching over the first. You can also zig-zag stitch back and forth a few times over the seam allowance of the slit and Tail to keep the fabric from fraying (see the photograph above).

SEWING INSTRUCTIONS FOR MONKEY

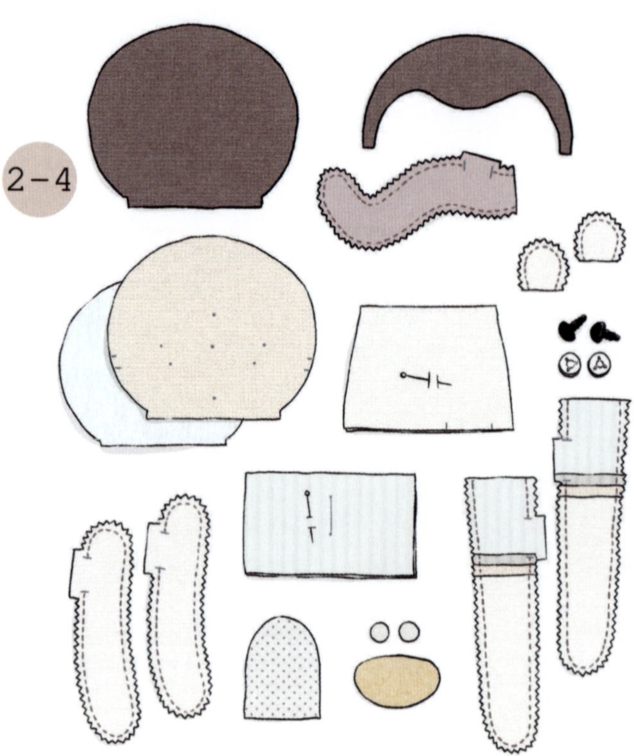

1. *Prepare fabric for Legs* – Cut a 9 x 5½in (23 x 14cm) piece of **Fabric A** and a 9 x 2¾in (23 x 7cm) piece of **Fabric C**. Lay **Fabric C** over **Fabric A** with right sides together and sew along the long side. Press seam open. Fold with right sides together so the shorter sides meet and press well.

2. *Transfer patterns and markings for all pieces as follows.* Take note of which fabric you'll be using for each piece and take care to transfer the correct lines as indicated: either the stitch line (without seam allowance) or the cutting line (with seam allowance included). When transferring stitch lines, be sure to leave ample space around the pattern pieces for the seam allowance.

On an 18 x 6in (46 x 15cm) piece of **Fabric A** which has been folded in half with right sides together so that you will have mirrored pieces, transfer Upper Body pattern on the cutting line. Once cut, transfer Tummy placement markings to the right side of fabric on Front piece and markings for opening on the wrong side of Back piece.

On the same piece of folded **Fabric A**, transfer Arm and Ear patterns twice each on stitch line. For Arms, transfer markings for openings to wrong side of fabric. Ears remain open at the bottom for turning.

On a 6½ x 6in (16.5 x 15cm) piece of **Fabric A**, transfer Head pattern on cutting line. This piece is Head Front (face). Transfer the face detail markings and appliqué and Ear placement markings to right side of fabric.

On a 6 x 5in (15 x 13cm) piece of **Fabric B** which has been folded in half with right sides together so that you will have mirrored pieces, transfer Tail pattern on stitch line. Transfer markings for opening. Note that the top also remains open.

On a 6¼ x 8in (16 x 20.5cm) piece of **Fabric B**, transfer the Head pattern on the cutting line. This piece is the Head Back. Transfer the Forehead pattern on the cutting line.

CONTINUES...

On a 10½ x 3¼in (26.5 x 8.5cm) piece of **Fabric C** which has been folded in half with right sides together so that you will have mirrored pieces, transfer Lower Body pattern on cutting line. Transfer slit placement markings to wrong side of fabric.

On the 2½ x 3in (6.5 x 7.5cm) piece of **Fabric D**, transfer Tummy pattern on cutting line.

On the **Fabric A/C** which has been folded in half with right sides together so that you will have mirrored pieces, position the Leg pattern carefully so that the seam matches up with the markings. Transfer Leg pattern twice on stitch line. Transfer markings for openings. The top of the Leg also remains open.

On **Felt A** and **B**, transfer all pieces on cutting line.

On the iron-on interfacing (optional), transfer Interfacing pattern on cutting line.

3. Cut out all pieces for which you transferred cutting lines.

4. ***Sew Arms, Legs, Ears and Tail*** – Sew directly on stitch lines, leaving openings as marked. Cut out around the sewing lines with pinking shears (see page 22). Turn pieces right side out and press out seams.

5. If using the optional iron-on interfacing, lay it on the wrong side of Head Front piece. Bond using the product's directions.

6. ***Prepare Ears*** – Fold each Ear in half. Starting at the bottom of the Ear, sew ½in (1.2cm) up along the fold, ⅛in (3mm) from the edge. Repeat for second Ear.

7. Add elbows to Arms and knees to Legs. See page 70.

8. ***Appliqué*** – Using markings, position appliqué pieces face up. Pin Forehead and Snout to right side of Head Front piece, and pin Tummy to right side of Upper Body piece. Appliqué pieces using directions on page 60 for Fabric Appliqué and page 46 for Felt Appliqué or page 30 for whipstitch.

9. ***Attach Eye pieces and doll eyes*** – With an Awl, ⅛in (3mm) hole punch or small scissors, make a small hole through the center of each (white felt) Eye piece and through the eye placement markings on Head Front piece. Because the felt pieces will be sandwiched between the doll eyes and the

6

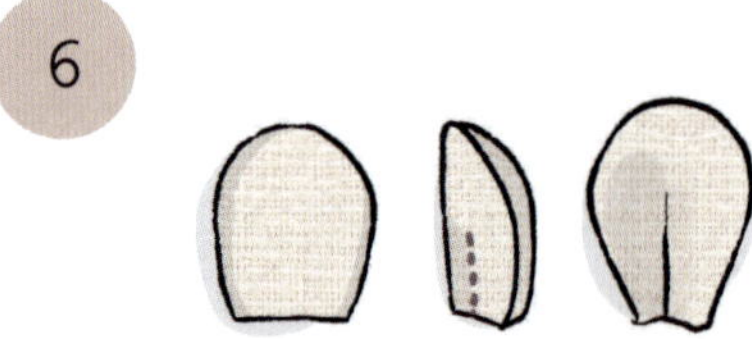

8

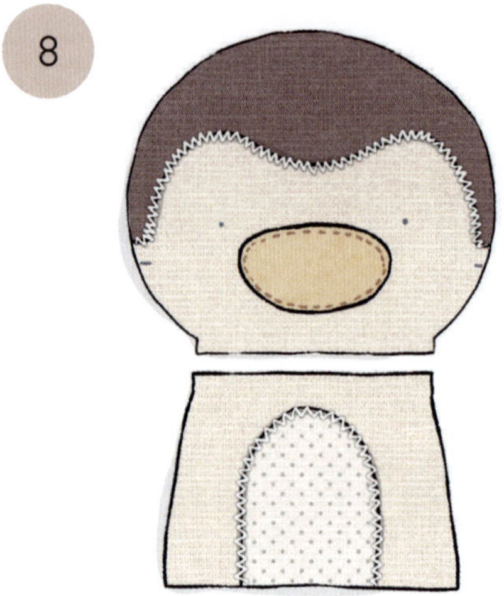

Head Front piece, they do not need to be sewn on. Insert the doll eye through the felt and fabric and secure with washer. Repeat for the other eye (see page 28).

10. *Embroider face details* – See Embroidery Stitches on pages 29–30. Using 3 strands of black embroidery floss, embroider the nose using a modified fly stitch and the mouth using straight stitch. Knot and cut floss. Once again with 3 strands of black embroidery floss, use straight stitches to create the eyelashes and eyebrows. If you are using light-colored fabric, trim the tails of the knots very short and hide the knots behind the felt of the eyes so that they don't show through the fabric.

11. Lay Upper Body pieces over Lower Body pieces with right sides together, making sure that you have correctly paired fronts and backs. Sew across, leaving opening as marked on the Back piece. Press open seams. These are now called Body pieces.

12. *Attach Tail* – See page 71.

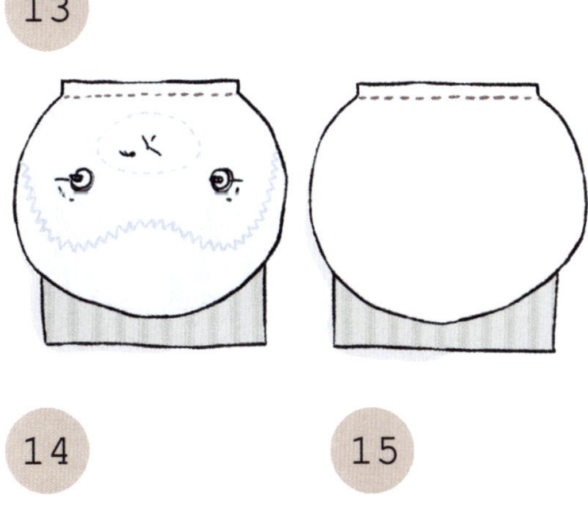

13. Lay Head pieces over Body pieces with right sides together, making sure that you have correctly paired fronts and backs. Sew across. These are now called Body pieces.

14. Using markings, position Ears on Body Front piece with right sides together. Pin or baste along edge to hold in place.

15. *Sew Body* – Lay Body Back piece over Body Front piece with right sides together and pin; either, fold the tail so that it emerges from the bottom opening or fold and pin it so that it won't get caught up in the side seams. Sew all the way around the body from the bottom edge on one side to the other side, leaving the bottom open. Reinforce seam on either side of neck with an extra line of stitching. Clip curves/ corners and trim seam allowance with pinking shears. Turn right side out and press out seams.

CONTINUES...

16. Turn the bottom edge of the Body under ½in (1.2cm) to the inside and press well to get a crisp crease. You can use a ruler and disappearing-ink pen to draw a line ½in (1.2cm) up from the bottom edge of the body on each side to ensure a straight and even fold.

17. Stuff the head firmly through the bottom opening. Stuff until just past the neck.

18. *Sew in Legs* – Insert Legs so that the top ½in (1.2cm) of each Leg is sandwiched inside the Body. Position them as far towards the sides of the Body as possible and be sure the toes are pointing inward. Pin or baste in place. Sew along the bottom edge ⅛in (3mm) from the edge. Run a second line of stitching over the first to ensure strength of seam. Remove basting stitches if necessary.

19. *Stuff and close* – Stuff Arms, Legs and Tail, then close with ladder stitch (see page 25).

20. Stuff the Body firmly, then close with ladder stitch.

21. Attach Arms to Body. See pages 26–27.

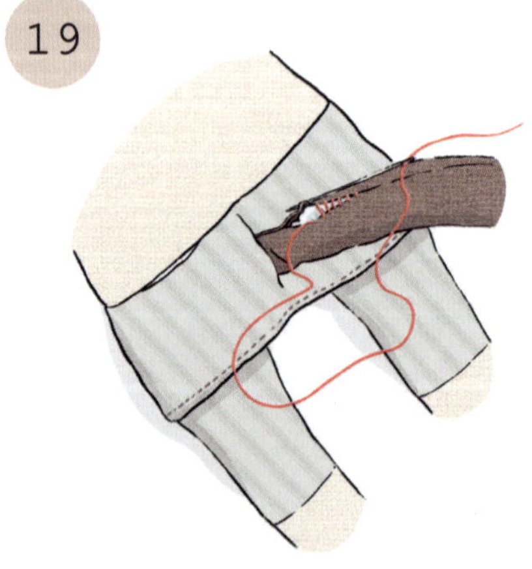

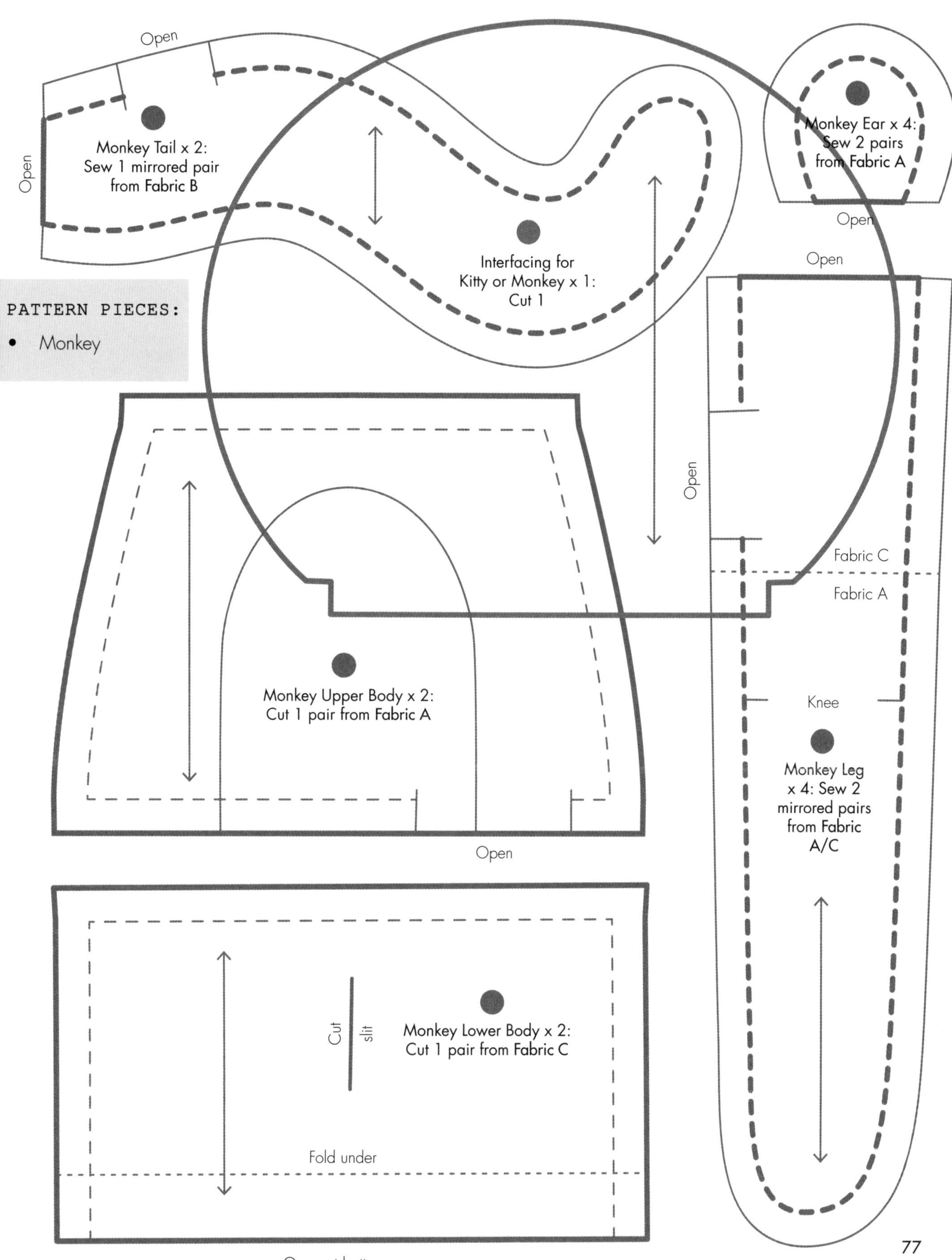

PATTERN PIECES:

- Monkey

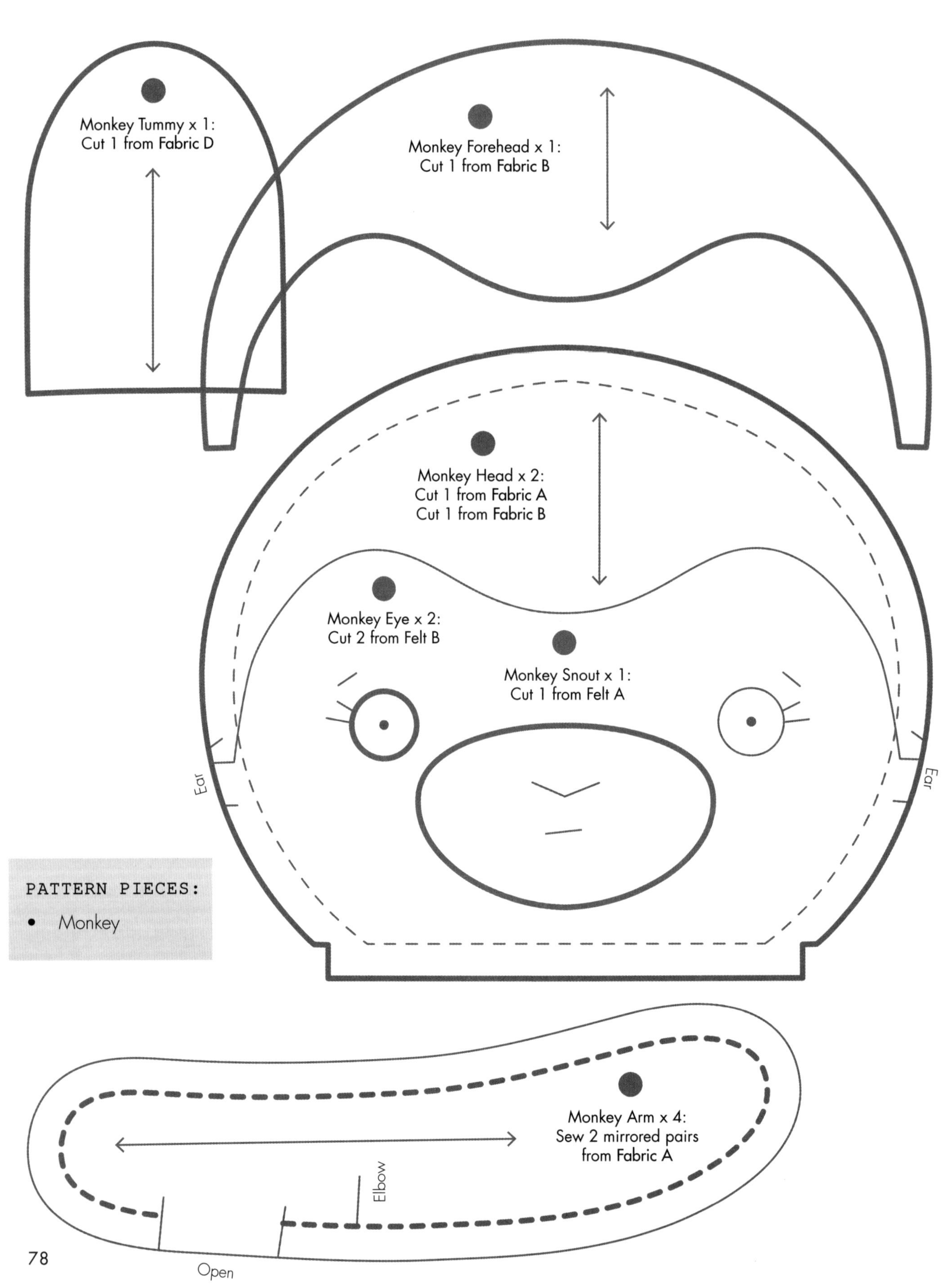

PATTERN PIECES:

- Monkey

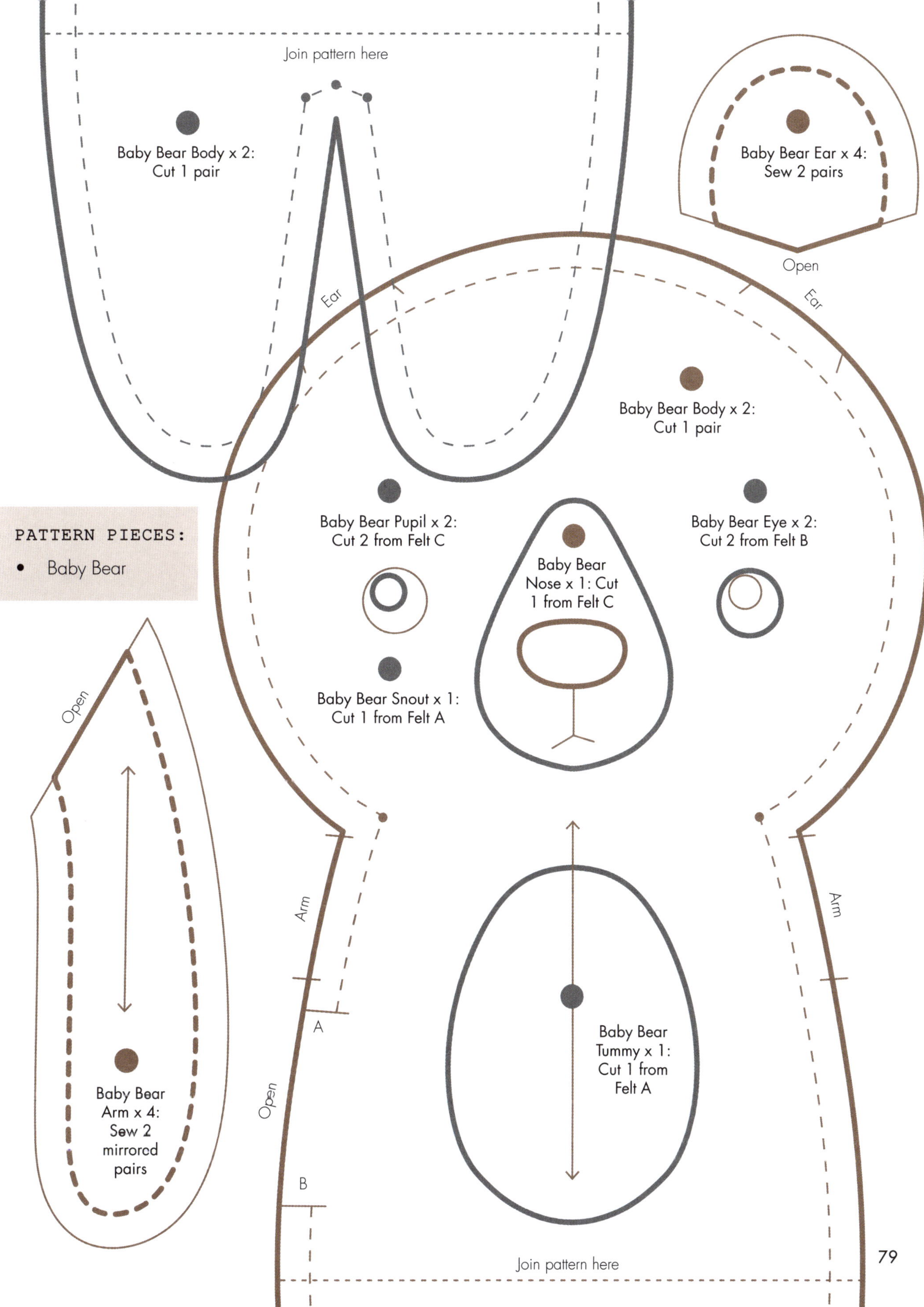
Join pattern here
Baby Bear Body x 2:
Cut 1 pair
Baby Bear Ear x 4:
Sew 2 pairs
Open
Ear
Ear
Baby Bear Body x 2:
Cut 1 pair
PATTERN PIECES:
• Baby Bear
Baby Bear Pupil x 2:
Cut 2 from Felt C
Baby Bear
Nose x 1: Cut
1 from Felt C
Baby Bear Eye x 2:
Cut 2 from Felt B
Baby Bear Snout x 1:
Cut 1 from Felt A
Open
Arm
Arm
A
Baby Bear
Tummy x 1:
Cut 1 from
Felt A
Baby Bear
Arm x 4:
Sew 2
mirrored
pairs
Open
B
Join pattern here

projects

SECTION TWO

In Section 1, we more or less stuck to the sandwich method of making dolls. Now that you've gained experience with embellishing dolls and manipulating a simple pattern, in this section we'll turn to the idea of adding dimensionality to our dolls. We'll explore several new construction methods and incorporate the use of darts, opening up a whole world of possibility for our designs.

You can think of our little Mouse doll as essentially the sandwich method that has been turned on its side. Rather than having a pattern piece for the front and back, it was made by designing the doll's profile, giving us side pieces with the seam running down the center of the face and body. This approach works particularly well with animals who have long and narrow heads, for example birds, horses, deer or, of course, mice. We'll also learn about darts and use them to add fullness to our Mouse's head.

SKILL LEVEL: BEGINNER

FINISHED SIZE: 8IN (20CM)

MATERIALS AND SPECIAL TOOLS FOR MOUSE

- Pattern pieces (see pages 15 and 106)
- **Fabric A**, medium-weight cotton or linen/cotton blend: 17 x 7¼in (43 x 44cm)
  - – Body x 2: Cut 1 mirrored pair
  - – Arm x 4: Sew 2 mirrored pairs
  - – Leg x 4: Sew 2 pairs
  - – Ear x 2: Sew 2 mirrored pairs from **Fabric A** and **B**
- **Fabric B**, medium-weight cotton or linen/cotton blend: 4 x 2in (10 x 5cm)
  - – Ear x 2: Sew 2 mirrored pairs from **Fabric A** and **B**
- Black gel fabric marker
- Embroidery floss in pink
- 4in (10cm) long piece of macrame cord, yarn, twine or ribbon for the Tail
- Doll needle and strong thread to attach arms
- Powder blush, beeswax crayon, colored pencil, or pink felt for cheeks (optional)

DARTS

You may be familiar with darts as they are typically used in clothing. Often found in the bust or hip area, they work to create volume in a flat, two-dimensional pieces of fabric. Similarly in doll-making, darts create roundness and dimensionality in a design.

A dart marking on a pattern looks like a triangle. The long dashed lines are the dart legs and the pointy end is the dart point. Some patterns also include the center line along which the fabric will be folded. A dart can have straight or curved dart legs.

TRANSFERRING DART MARKINGS TO FABRIC

Dart markings are always transferred to the wrong side of the fabric. There are two ways to transfer dart markings to your fabric. The first method works well for darts with straight legs and the second is better for darts with curved legs.

For the ***first method***, transfer the markings for the dart point and the place where each dart leg meets the edge of the fabric. Then draw the dart legs onto the fabric by connecting the dots with a ruler (see the illustration, opposite).

For the ***second method***, cut the paper pattern piece along each curved dart leg, stopping at the dart point. Cutting the pattern piece allows us to use it as a stencil along which to trace the dart onto the fabric (see the illustration, opposite). Take note: when transferring a pattern with the dart cut out, I recommend that you draw a line connecting the two dart legs along what will be the edge of the fabric. This line provides a guide for cutting out the fabric piece and helps us avoid accidentally cutting along the dart legs.

HOW TO SEW A DART

1. Begin by pinching the fabric with right sides together so that it folds along the center of the dart (on the center line if one was provided) and through the dart point. Because the dart is sewn directly on the dart legs, it's important that both legs match up exactly. Double check the alignment by poking a pin through the dart leg on one side and turning the fabric around to verify that the pin comes out exactly on the marked dart leg on the other side. Press the fold and pin to hold.

2. Starting at the top of the dart leg at the edge of the fabric, sew towards the dart point. Secure the beginning of the seam with backstitch. Sew directly on the dart leg until just before the dart point, then taper your stitching a bit by angling your stitch line to run almost parallel to the edge of the fold for a couple stitches as you reach the dart point. Sew right to the edge of the fabric with your last stitch as close to the edge as possible. Do not backstitch to secure and do not cut the thread. Gently pull the piece from your sewing machine until the thread tails are about 5in (13cm) long. Take care not to pull too hard or it may cause the fabric to pucker. Secure the seam by tying a double knot. Trim thread tails to about ¼in (6mm).

3. A dart's seam allowance is typically pressed toward the back or bottom, unless otherwise stated in the pattern. If necessary, clip off the tip of the seam allowance at an angle so that it doesn't protrude past the edge of the fabric.

A note on stuffing: When stuffing a doll with darts, be sure to push filler firmly into the dart seam and to fully stuff the area, especially at the dart point. This will ensure that the full curvature and shape of the dart is expressed.

FIRST METHOD

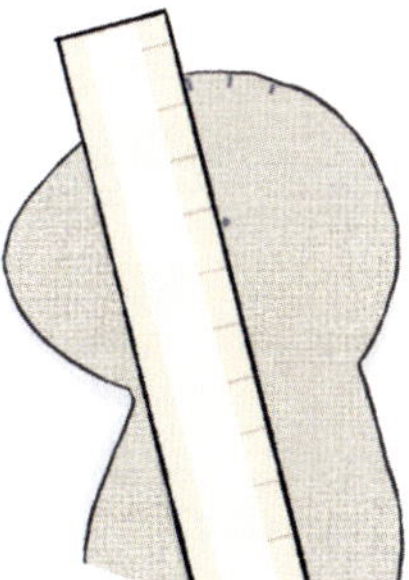

SECOND METHOD

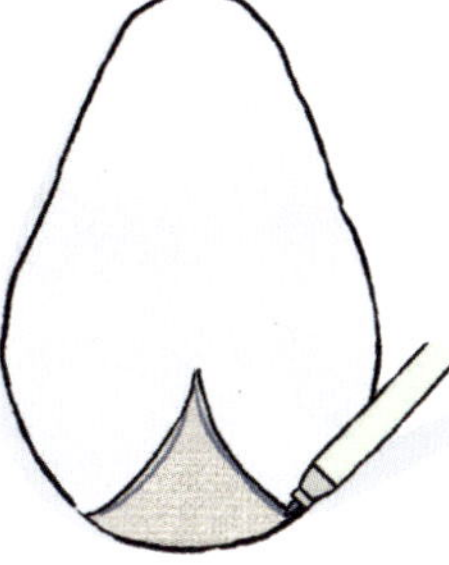

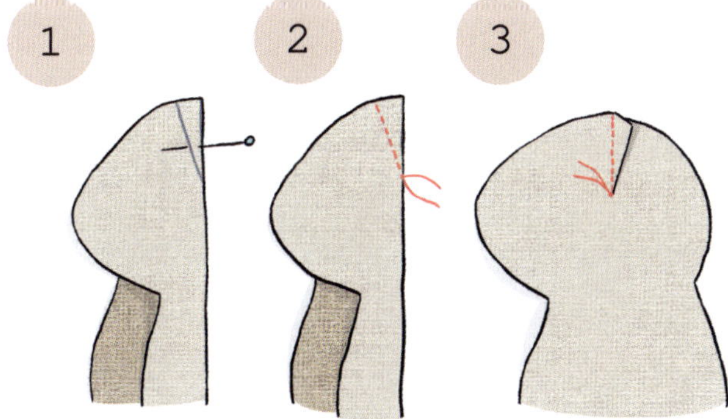

DESIGNING WITH DARTS

- Darts can be placed anywhere on a pattern where you'd like to create volume and roundness.
- When adding a dart to an existing pattern, in order to maintain the size of the pattern piece, you must compensate for the fabric that is sewn into the dart by adding length or width to the pattern which is equal to the dart width.
- The wider the dart (the farther apart the dart legs) the more fullness it will create and the farther it will protrude.
- To keep a dart from protruding from the fabric in an undesirable way, use curved dart legs to create roundness and avoid pointiness.
- The longer the dart (the farther the dart point is from the edge of the fabric) the gentler the curve will be.
- It's important to find an appropriate balance of width and length in order to achieve your desired effect.

ATTACHING EARS WITH LADDER STITCH

Most of the patterns in this book include placement markings or suggestions indicating where to position ears, but feel free to experiment. You will find that the position and curvature of a doll's ears will have a very big impact on their look and personality.

1. Once you have found a position you like, pin the ears to the head at each corner and use one or two pins along the base of the ear to create the desired curvature (see the photograph above left). Look at your doll from all sides to ensure that both sides are symmetrical.

2. Thread your needle with strong thread and tie a knot. Trim the end close to the knot. Insert your needle into the underside of the ear at one corner, hiding the knot under the ear. Make several small stitches at the corner to secure.

3. Ladder stitch across the back side using very small, even stitches, alternating between the bottom edge of the ear and the head (see page 25 for how to work ladder stitch). Pull the stitches gently as you go. Once you've reached the other corner, make several small stitches to secure, then turn your doll around and ladder stitch across the front of the ear (see the photograph above right). If the doll is intended for play, I suggest you circle the ear again with another round of ladder stitch.

4. To finish, knot under the ear to secure. Reinsert the needle right next to the knot, then come out as far away as you can. Pull firmly on the thread to sink the knot and hide it under the ear. Trim the thread tail close to the fabric and let it disappear back into the doll.

5. Double-check the position of the second ear, adjusting if necessary. Repeat steps 2–4 for second ear.

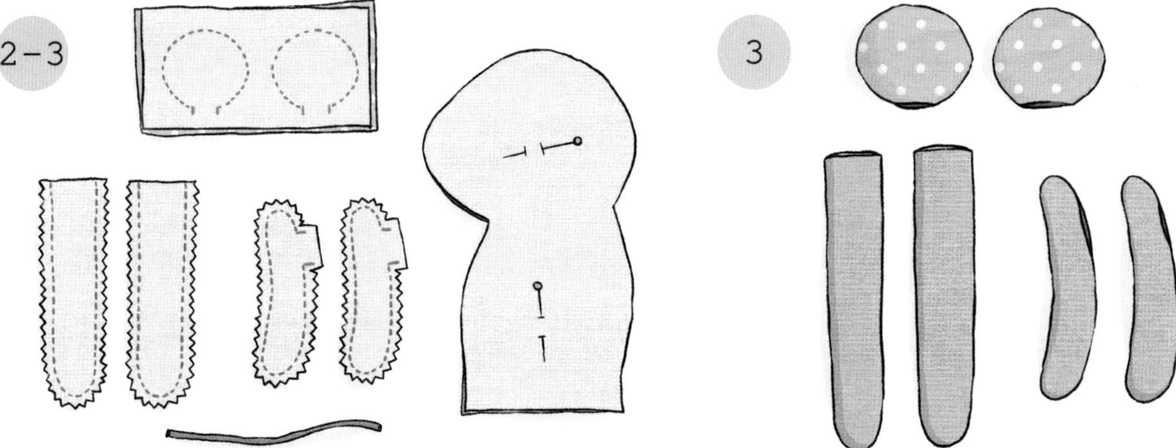

1. *Transfer patterns and markings for all pieces as follows*. Take care to transfer the correct lines as indicated: either the stitch line (without seam allowance) or the cutting line (with seam allowance included). When transferring stitch lines, be sure to leave ample space around the pattern pieces for seam allowance.

On a 17 X 7¼in (43 x 18.5cm) piece of **Fabric A** which has been folded in half with right sides together so that you will have mirrored pieces, transfer Body pattern on cutting line. Once cut, transfer opening markings to wrong side of top piece and dart markings to wrong side of both pieces. Transfer Tail placement marking to right side of bottom piece. Transfer markings for eye placement to right side of both pieces, or if you prefer, you can wait and decide on the eye placement after the head has been stuffed.

On the same piece of folded **Fabric A**, transfer Arm and Leg patterns twice each on stitch line. For Arm, transfer markings for opening placement to wrong side of fabric. The top of the Leg remains open

Cut a 4 x 2in (10 x 5cm) piece each of **Fabrics A** and **B**. Lay one over the other with right sides together and transfer Ear pattern twice on stitch line. Transfer markings for opening placement to wrong side of fabric.

2. Cut out Body pieces.

3. *Sew Arms, Legs and Ears* – Sew directly on stitch line, leaving openings as marked. Cut out around the sewing line, using pinking shears, except at openings (see page 22). Turn right side out and press out seams.

CONTINUES...

4. *Darts* – Sew darts on Body pieces (see pages 84–85). Clip off tip of dart seam allowance at an angle. Press seam allowance towards the back of the head.

5. *Tail* – Baste tail to right side of one body piece at marking.

6. *Sew Body* – Lay Body pieces with right sides together, aligning dart seams at the top of the head. Pin together, leaving bottom edge open with the tail poking out to keep it out of the way of the stitching. Sew all the way around from bottom edge to bottom edge, leaving marked opening and bottom open. Reinforce the seam at the tail and both sides of the neck with an extra line of stitching. Clip curves and trim seam allowance with pinking shears. Turn right side out and press out seams.

7. Turn the bottom edge of the Body under ½in (1.2cm) to the inside. You can use a ruler and disappearing-ink pen to draw a line ½in (1.2cm) up from the bottom edge of the body on each side to ensure a straight and even fold. Now realign the bottom edges so that center seams meet. Press well to get a crisp crease.

8. *Stuff Head* – Stuff firmly through either the bottom or back opening until just past the neck.

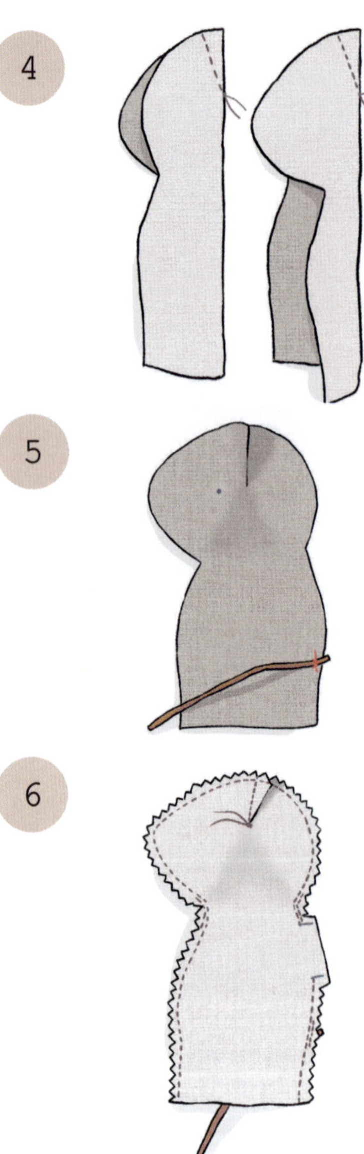

CONTINUES...

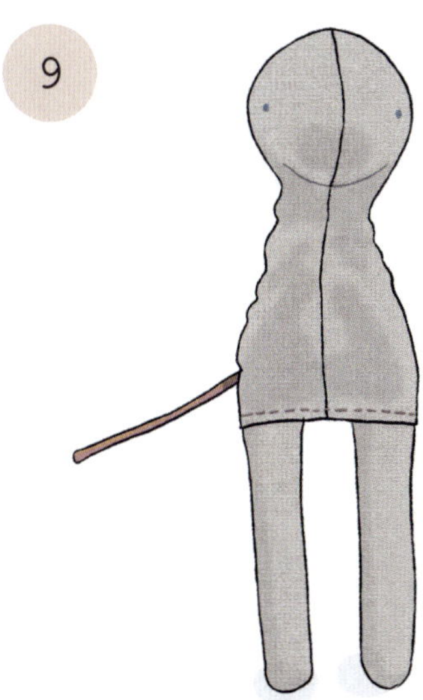

9. *Attach Legs* – Stuff Legs to ½in (1.2cm) from the top opening. Insert Legs through the bottom opening of the Body so that the top ⅜in (1cm) of each Leg is sandwiched inside. Position the Legs as far towards the sides of the Body as possible. Pin or baste in place to secure. Sew along the bottom edge of the Body ⅛in (3mm) from the folded edge. Run an additional line of stitching over the first to ensure strength of seam. Remove basting stitches if necessary.

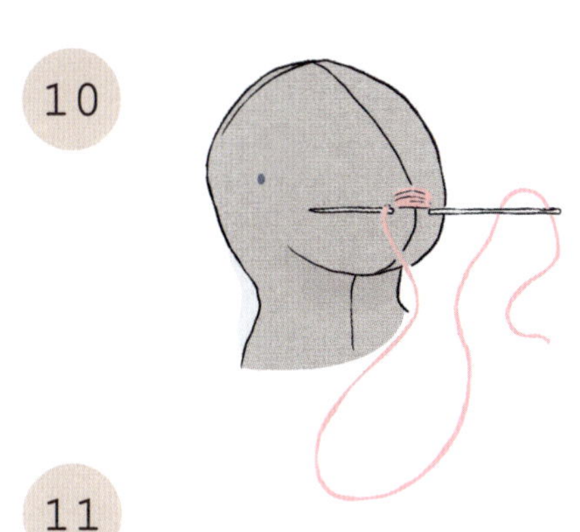

10. *Embroider face details* – see Embroidery Stitches on pages 29–30. Draw in face details with disappearing-ink pen to provide a stitch guide. Thread a doll needle with 3 strands of pink embroidery floss. Insert the needle through the opening in the back, emerging at the nose. Use satin stitch to create the nose.

11. Make the mouth using the same piece of embroidery floss by bringing the needle out about ¼in (6mm) below the nose on the seam. Use the center seam as a guide to make sure the needle is centered. Insert the needle about ¼in (6mm) down and ⅛in (3mm) to the left, emerging in the same spot on the right side of the center seam. Complete the second stitch by re-inserting the needle into the same spot in the center seam where we began the first mouth stitch. Emerge and knot off thread where it will be covered by an Ear or Arm.

12. Draw eyes and eyebrows with fabric marker.

13. *Stuff and close Body* – Continue stuffing the neck and body until packed firmly then close with ladder stitch (see page 25).

14. Stuff Arms then close with ladder stitch.

15. *Attach Ears* – With **Fabric B** facing forward, position Ears so that the inner base of the Ear is around ¾in (2cm) below the center seam and about ½in (1.2cm) behind the dart seams. Pin in place and attach with ladder stitch (see page 86).

16. *Attach Arms* – Position Arms over side seams. Take care when pinning Arms in place – because our Mouse is so little, the pins will come through to the other side if pushed in all the way. Don't poke yourself! Attach Arms to Body (see pages 26–27).

The Fox doll combines the front and back construction we used in Section 1 with the side to side approach we took with the Mouse. By dividing the front into two pieces, we are able to achieve the distinctly fox-like shape of a broad forehead in combination with a long and narrow muzzle. A dart at the back of the head rounds out the shape and provides balance to the design.

SKILL LEVEL: CONFIDENT BEGINNER

FINISHED SIZE: 14½IN (37CM)

MATERIALS AND SPECIAL TOOLS FOR FOX

- Pattern pieces (see inside-back cover and page 15)
- **Fabric A**, medium-weight cotton or linen/cotton blend: 15½ x 17in (39.5 x 43cm)
    - – Head x 2: Cut 1 mirrored pair
    - – Front Body x 2: Cut 1 mirrored pair
    - – Back Body x 1: Cut 1
- **Fabric B**, medium-weight cotton or linen/cotton blend: 6½ x 8½in (16.5 x 21.5cm)
    - – Appliqué x 2: Cut 1 mirrored pair
- **Fabric C**, medium-weight cotton or linen/cotton blend:13 x 6in (33 x 15cm)
    - – Foot x 4: Cut 2 mirrored pairs
- **Fabric A/C**:
    - – Arm x 4: Sew 2 mirrored pairs
- **Fabric B** and **C**: 5 x 3in (13 x 7.5cm) each
    - – Ear x 4: Sew 2 mirrored pairs
- Woven iron-on interfacing (optional): 9 x 9in (23 x 23cm)
    - – Interfacing x 2: Cut 1 mirrored pair
- Embroidery floss in black
- Doll needle and strong thread to attach arms
- Powder blush, beeswax crayon, colored pencil, or pink felt for cheeks (optional)

SEWING INSTRUCTIONS FOR FOX

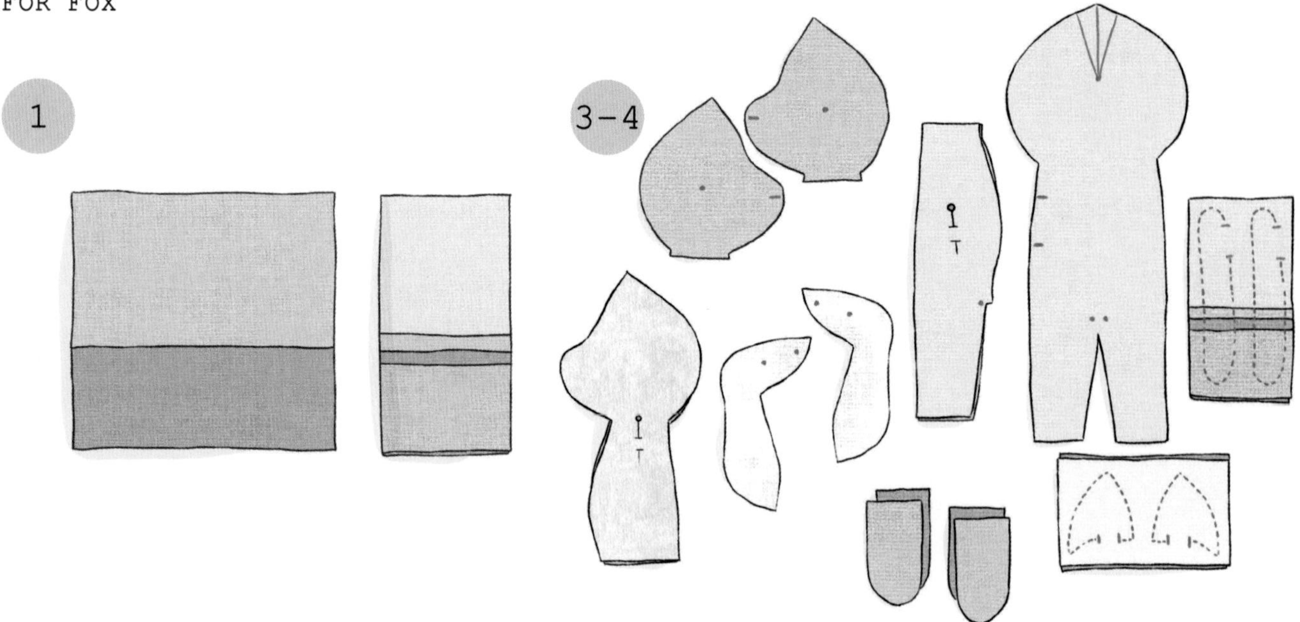

1. *Prepare fabric for Arms* – Cut a 6 x 3¾in (15 x 9.5cm) piece of **Fabric A** and a 6 x 2½in (15 x 6.5cm) piece of **Fabric C**. Lay **Fabric C** over **Fabric A** with right sides together and sew along the long side. Press seam open. Fold with right sides together so shorter sides meet and press well.

2. *Transfer patterns and markings for all pieces as follows*. Take note of which fabric you'll be using for each piece and take care to transfer the correct lines as indicated: either the stitch line (without seam allowance) or the cutting line (with seam allowance included). When transferring stitch lines, be sure to leave ample space around the pattern pieces for seam allowance.

On a 9½ x 14½in (24 x 37cm) piece of **Fabric A** which has been folded in half with right sides together so that you will have mirrored pieces, transfer Head pattern on cutting line. Once cut, transfer eye and appliqué placement markings to right sides of fabric. Transfer Front Body pattern on cutting line. Transfer B marking to wrong side.

On a 6 x 13¼in (15 x 33.5cm) piece of **Fabric A**, transfer Back Body pattern on cutting line. Transfer markings for dart, opening and crotch to wrong side of fabric.

On a 6½ x 5½in (16.5 x 14cm) piece of **Fabric B** which has been folded in half with right sides together so that you will have mirrored pieces, transfer Appliqué pattern on cutting line. Once cut, transfer markings to right sides of fabric.

On an 8½ x 3½in (21.5 x 9cm) piece of **Fabric C** which has been folded in half with right sides together so that you will have mirrored pieces, transfer Foot pattern twice on cutting line.

On the prepared **Fabric A/C** which has been folded in half with right sides together so that you will have mirrored pieces, transfer Arm pattern twice on stitch line. Position the pattern piece carefully so that the seam matches up with the markings. Transfer markings for opening placement to wrong side of fabric.

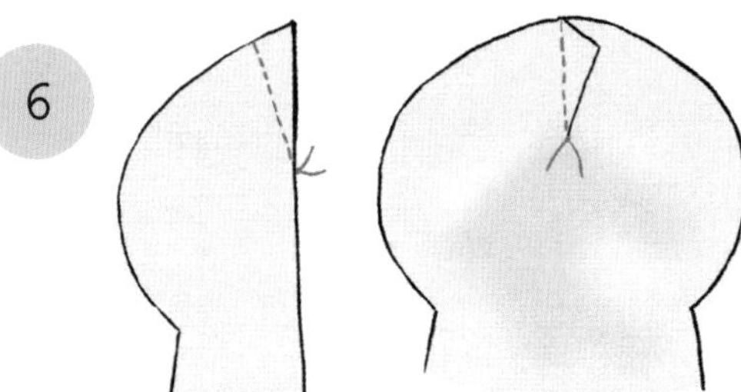

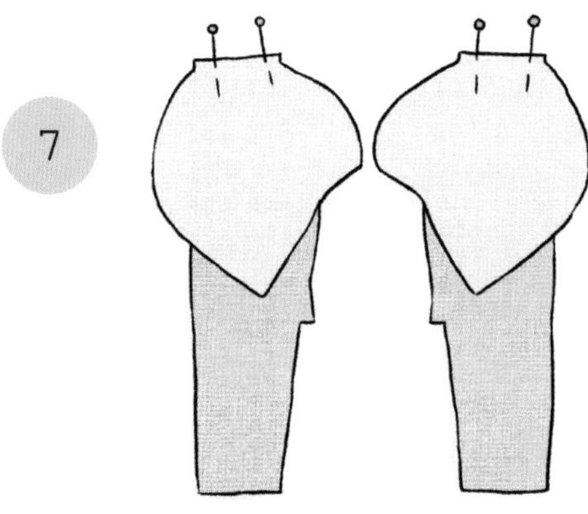

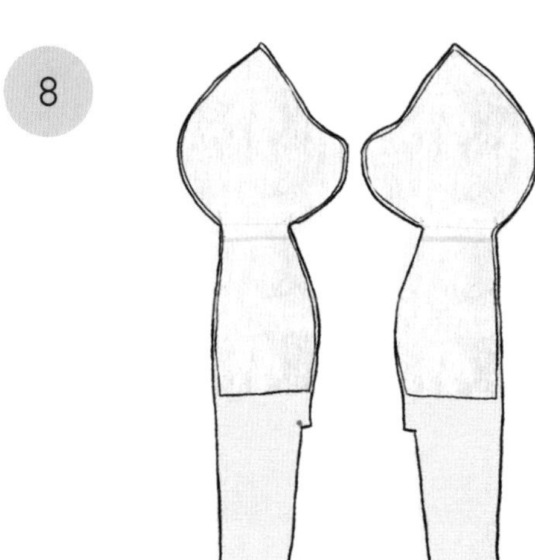

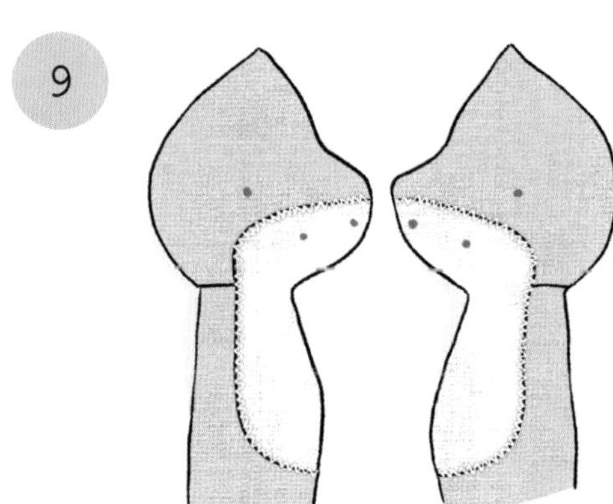

Cut a 5 x 3in (13 x 7.5cm) piece each of **Fabrics B** and **C**. Lay one over the other with right sides together and transfer Ear pattern twice on the stitch line, flipping over the pattern piece for the second Ear so that you will have a mirrored set as shown in the illustration. Transfer markings for opening placement to wrong side of fabric.

On the iron-on interfacing (optional) which has been folded in half with wrong sides together (but not ironed) so that you will have mirrored pieces, transfer the Interfacing pattern on the cutting line.

3. Cut out all pieces for which you transferred cutting lines.

4. *Sew Arms and Ears directly on stitch line*. Leave openings as marked. Cut out around the sewing line, using pinking shears except at openings (see page 22). For Ears, clip off corner points at a diagonal and trim seam allowance very close to the stitching line leading up to the corners.

5. *Prepare Ears* – Turn Ears right side out and press out seams, paying special attention to points. Ladder stitch Ears closed (see page 25). Ears are not stuffed.

6. *Sew dart on Back Body piece.* Clip off tip of seam allowance at an angle so that it doesn't protrude past the edge of the fabric. Press seam to the right.

7. Lay Head pieces over Front Body pieces with right sides together, making sure that you have correctly paired left and right sides. Sew across, then press open seams. These are now called Front Body pieces.

8. If using the optional iron-on interfacing, align Interfacing pieces over wrong sides of Front Body pieces. Bond using the product's directions.

9. *Appliqué* – Using markings to position, pin Appliqué pieces (right side facing up) to right side of Front Body pieces, aligning carefully along the edge. Appliqué using zig-zag stitch along the interior edge (see page 60).

CONTINUES...

10. *Join Front Body pieces* – Pin the two Front Body pieces together with right sides facing. Sew from A to B. Clip curves with pinking shears and press open seams. The two joined pieces will now be called Front Body.

11. Pin Foot pieces to legs on Front and Back Body pieces with right sides together. Make sure the toes point in. Sew in place. Press open seams.

12. *Sew Body* – Lay Back Body piece over Front Body piece with right sides together, aligning at top center, neck and ankle seams. Pin together carefully. Note that the front and back pieces are not the same width so align carefully along the sides. Sew all the way around the body, pivoting at crotch markings, leaving an opening as marked. Reinforce seam at neck and crotch with an extra line of stitching. Clip curves and corners with pinking shears. Turn right side out and press out seams.

13. Stuff the body firmly, making sure to fill the snout completely. Use ladder stitch to close the opening (see page 25).

14. *Embroider face details* – See Embroidery Stitches on pages 29–30. The same continuous piece of floss will be used for all face details, so make sure it is plenty long – at least 30in (76cm). Thread a long doll needle with 3 strands of black embroidery floss. To begin, insert the needle where the knot will later be covered by an ear or arm or use the "pop it through" method to hide the knot (see page 31). Emerge at the nose and use satin stitch to embroider the nose.

15. Emerge centered just below the satin-stitched nose. Make a long stitch straight down and insert the needle at the center marking. Emerge at the marking on the left. Slide the needle under the center stitch and insert at the marking on the right, creating the mouth.

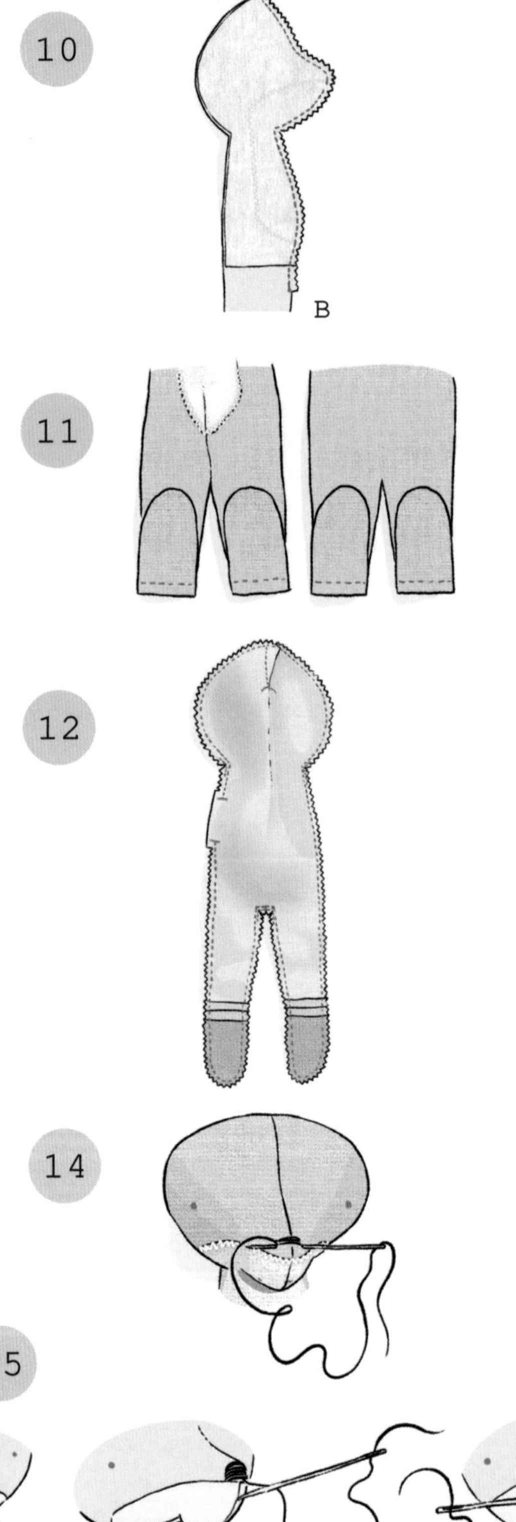

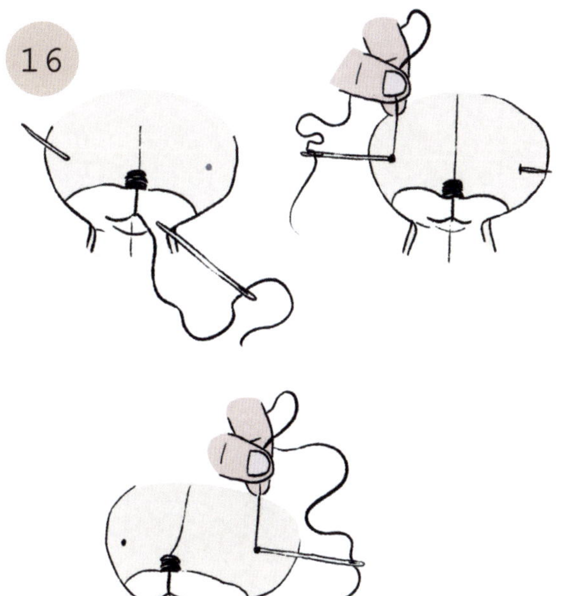

16. Emerge at eye marking. Make the eye with a French knot, emerging at the eye marking on the other side. I wound the thread around my needle four times for each French knot. Make the second eye, then emerge and knot off the thread where it will be covered by an ear or arm.

17. *Attach Ears* – With **Fabric B** facing forward, position the Ears directly over the seam and attach with ladder stitch (see page 25).

18. *Attach Arms* – Turn Arms right side out and press out seams. Stuff and close with ladder stitch. Position Arms at side seam about ½in (1.2cm) down from neck seam. Attach Arms to Body (see pages 26–27).

dog

How could I ever express my love of dogs – or their love for us – through one little doll? With these soulful eyes, floppy ears, expressive eyebrows and the sweetest round belly, I hope I've managed to capture a bit of their delightful and endearing nature. Design-wise, the head is constructed with four pieces – two each for the front and back – a construction method that gives us the ability to achieve a great variety of shapes with a lot of nuance. Darts are used in the body to create the rounded tummy. The head and body are separate forms which are fitted one into the other and attached with ladder stitch after they've been stuffed. The legs are also ladder-stitched to the body.

SKILL LEVEL: CONFIDENT BEGINNER

FINISHED SIZE: 10½IN (26.5CM)

MATERIALS AND SPECIAL TOOLS FOR DOG

- Pattern pieces (see pages 15 and 106–107)
- **Fabric A**, medium-weight cotton or linen/cotton blend: 19 x 12½in (48 x 32cm)
    - Head Front x 2: Cut/sew 1 mirrored pair
    - Head Back x 2: Cut/sew 1 mirrored pair
    - Body x 2: Cut 1 pair
    - Arm x 4: Sew 2 mirrored pairs
    - Leg x 4: Sew 2 mirrored pairs
    - Ear x 4: Sew 2 mirrored pairs
- Doll needle and strong thread
- Embroidery Floss in black, brown, and white
- Embroidery Floss in a color just a bit darker than fabric color for eyebrows (optional)
- Powder blush, beeswax crayon, colored pencil, or pink felt for cheeks (optional)

ATTACHING HEAD TO BODY WITH LADDER STITCH

These instructions refer to the Dog pattern in which the Body is inserted into the Head and then the two forms are sewn together. I've also included notes here for the Bear pattern (page 124) in which the Head and Body are two separate closed forms sewn together.

1. Insert the neck as far into the Head as possible, removing some stuffing from the Head if necessary to make it fit. Draw out the fabric at the opening of the Head so that the creased folds make a sort of socket around the neck area. Tweezers or a hemostat can help to draw out and position the fabric neatly and evenly around the neck.
2. Make any adjustments to the position of the Head on the Body. Look at it from all sides to ensure the Head is straight or at your preferred angle.
3. Pin Head in place. Insert pins through the socket/ base of the Head, angling them upwards so that they go through the neck portion of the body and up into the Head. ***Be careful*** – if the pins are not angled upward, they may come out the other side and poke you.
4. For the Bear, insert pins through the chest, angling them upwards into the Head. You may choose to draw a circle with a disappearing-ink pen around the base of the Bear's Head and a corresponding line at the top of the Body where the forms meet. This will give you a line to guide your stitching.
5. Using strong thread for a secure attachment, insert your needle under the socket at the center of the Head opening on the back side. Ladder stitch all the way around the head along the base of the socket or along the marked lines for the Bear. Use very small even stitches, alternating one stitch on the Head and one stitch on the Body. (See page 25 for how to work ladder stitch.)
6. Circle the head several times, pulling the stitches firmly as you go, but not so tightly that it causes the fabric to pucker. On each subsequent round, bring your stitches a tiny bit further out – lower on the Body, and higher on the Head. Small, even stitches will make the attachment strong, clean and almost invisible.
7. Knot on the backside to secure, then reinsert the needle next to the knot, under the seam, and come out as far away as you can. Pull firmly on the thread to sink the knot and hide it under the seam. Trim the thread tail close to the fabric and let it disappear back into the doll. For the Bear, hide knots between the Head and Body.

ATTACHING LEGS TO BODY WITH LADDER STITCH

1. Position the Legs along the bottom seam of the Body and pin in place from the front and back. Hold up the doll and look from all sides to ensure that you like the placement. If the Legs are mirrored, make sure they are on the correct sides and facing forward (if applicable).

2. Using strong thread for a secure attachment, insert your needle into the inner corner of one Leg so that your knot will be hidden between the Leg and Body. Ladder stitch around the Leg on both the front and back, alternating small, even stitches between the top edge of the Leg and the Body. Circle the Leg several times, pulling the stitches firmly as you go, but not so tightly that the fabric puckers.

3. Knot on the backside to secure, then reinsert the needle next to the knot and come out as far away as you can. Pull firmly on the thread to sink the knot and hide it between the Leg and Body. Trim the thread tail close to the fabric and let it disappear back into the doll. Repeat for the second leg.

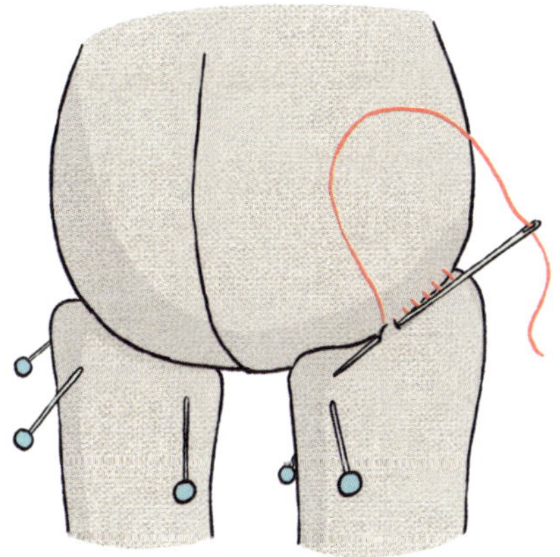

SEWING INSTRUCTIONS
FOR DOG

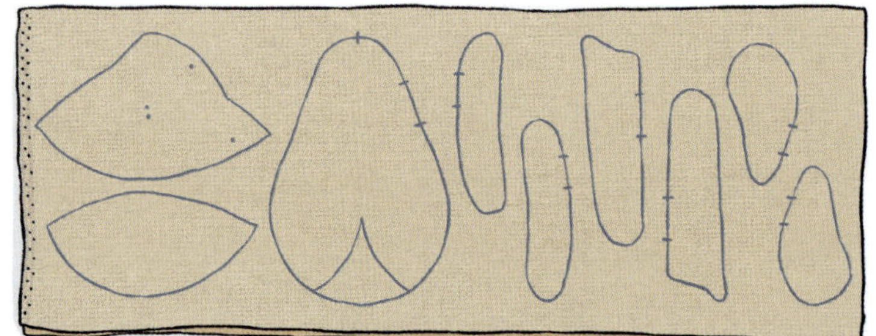

1. *Transfer all pattern pieces* to the 19 x 12½in (48 x 32cm) piece of **Fabric A** which has been folded in half with right sides together so that you will have mirrored pieces. Take care to transfer the correct lines as indicated: either the stitch line (without seam allowance) or the cutting line (with seam allowance included). When transferring stitch lines, be sure to leave ample space around the pattern pieces.

   Pay careful attention to the grainline when laying out Head Front and Head Back pieces. For both pieces, transfer the stitch line for the center-front or center-back seam and the cutting line for the remaining edge (see illustration 6A). Transfer all markings to wrong side of fabric. Later we will transfer them to the right side using the pin method after the pieces have been cut out.

   Transfer Body pattern on cutting line. Transfer all markings to wrong side of fabric. If you have cut the dart out of the pattern piece, it's useful to mark a line on your fabric connecting the two dart legs along what will be the edge of your fabric.

   Transfer Arm, Leg and Ear patterns twice each on stitch line. Transfer markings for opening placement to wrong side of fabric on each piece.

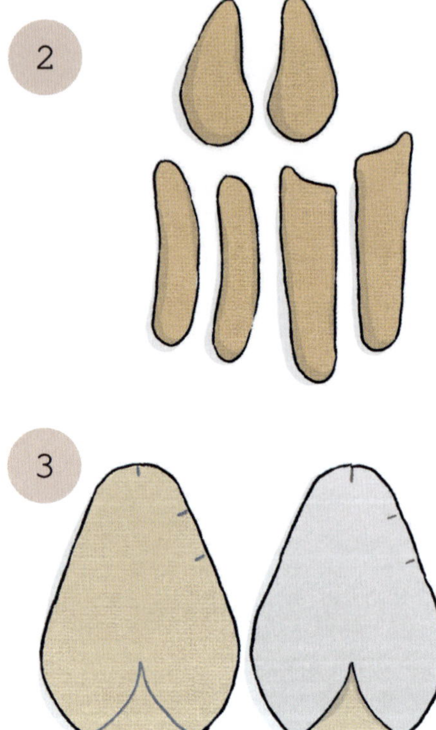

2. *Sew Arms, Legs and Ears* – Sew directly on stitch line, leaving openings as marked. Cut out around the sewing lines with pinking shears (see page 22). Turn all pieces right side out and press out seams. Stuff Arms and Legs and close with ladder stitch. Ladder stitch Ears closed; they are not stuffed.

3. Cut out Body pieces. Take care not to cut along dart lines! Transfer top center and dart markings to wrong side of second piece.

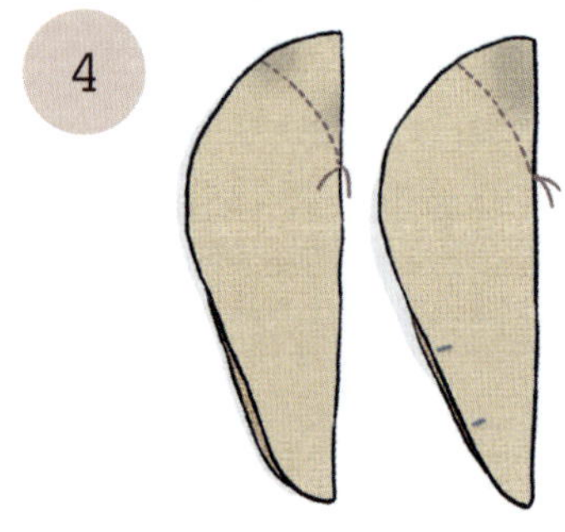

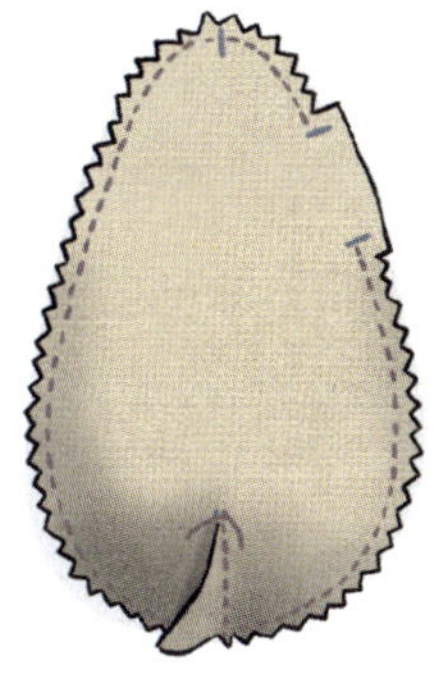

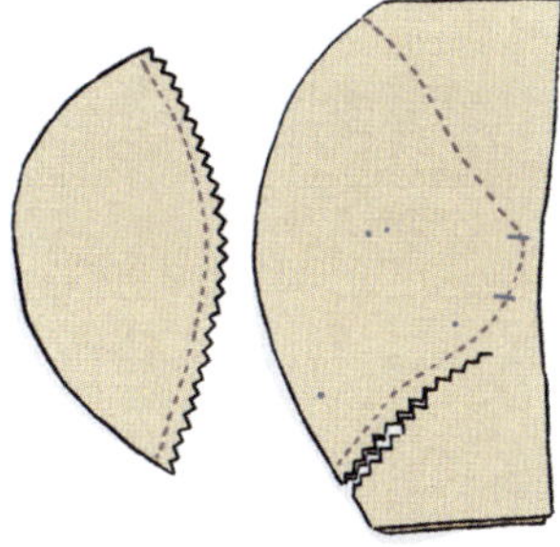

6B

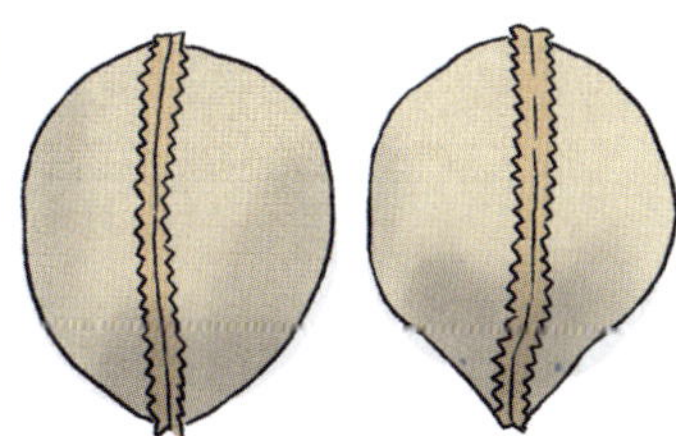

7

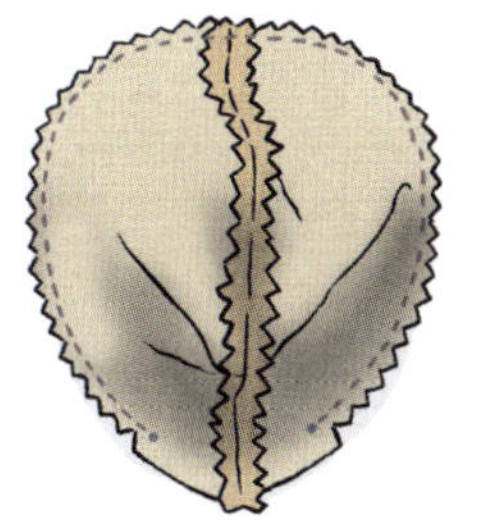

4. ***Sew darts*** on Body pieces along curved dart legs. Clip off tip of dart seam allowance at an angle. Press seam allowance to the right.

5. ***Sew Body*** – With right sides together, align Body pieces at top center markings and dart seams. Sew all the way around the body, leaving an opening as marked. Clip curves/trim seams with pinking shears. Turn right side out and press out seams.

6. For both Head Front and Head Back, sew center-front/center-back seam of pieces only, directly on stitch line. Cut out pieces using regular scissors to cut on the cut lines and pinking shears to cut close to the stitch lines (see illustration 6A). For Head Front, use the pin method to transfer the markings for the opening to wrong side of bottom piece and face detail markings to both right sides (see page 17). Or, you may prefer to draw face details in later freehand. Open up pieces and press open seams (see illustration 6B).

7. Lay Head Front piece over Head Back piece with right sides together, aligning center seams at top and bottom. Sew around, leaving an opening at the bottom as marked. Being sure to leave the seam allowance at the opening uncut, clip curves/trim seams with pinking shears. Turn right side out and press out seams. Neatly tuck in the seam allowance at the opening and press well to get a crisp crease.

8. ***Stuff Head and Body***. Take special care to stuff the neck and shoulder area very firmly to make a solid base to which you'll attach the Head. Ladder stitch Body closed (see page 25). Leave opening in Head.

CONTINUES...

9. *Embroider face details* – See Embroidery Stitches on pages 29–30. Using markings as your guide, draw in face details with disappearing-ink pen – eyes, eyebrows, nose and mouth. Using black embroidery floss, insert the doll needle through the opening at the bottom of the head, emerging at the nose. Use satin stitch to embroider the nose (see 9A). Then, use backstitch to outline the eyes and satin stitch to fill them in (see 9B). Tie off knot on the side of the head where it will later be hidden by an ear.

10. With white embroidery floss, use French knots or a few straight stitches to create the highlight in the eyes.

11. With brown embroidery floss, use backstitch to embroider the mouth. Begin stitching directly below the nose and stitch down along the center seam for approximately ¾in (2cm). Each side of the mouth is about ¾in (2cm) long and ends approximately ⅜in (1cm) from center seam.

12. Continue with brown embroidery floss or switch to a color that more closely matches the fabric color. Use backstitch to outline the eyebrows.

13. *Assembly* – Ladder stitch Head to Body (see page 100).

14. Ladder stitch Legs to Body (see page 101).

15. Position Arms at side seam about ¼in (6mm) down from neck seam. Attach Arms to Body (see pages 26–27).

16. Position Ears on seam 1½–1¾in (4–4.5cm) down from top center of the Head. Ears can be attached with the same method(s) used to attach arms, or they can be ladder-stitched to the head around the top of the ear.

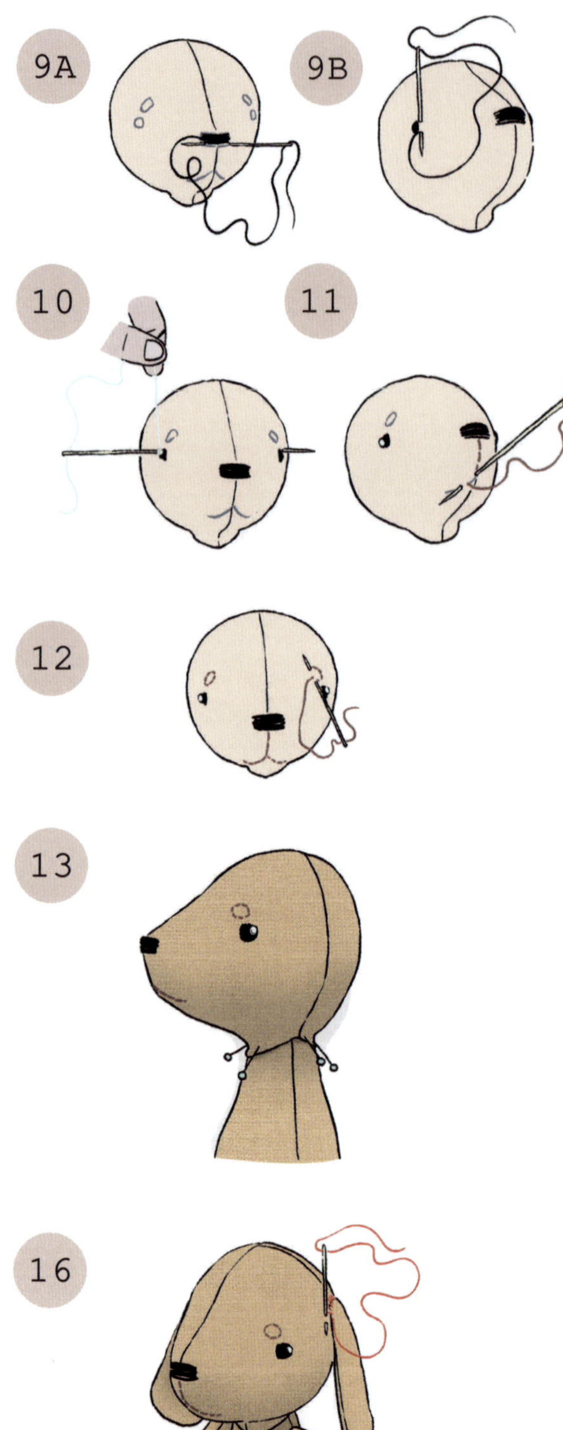

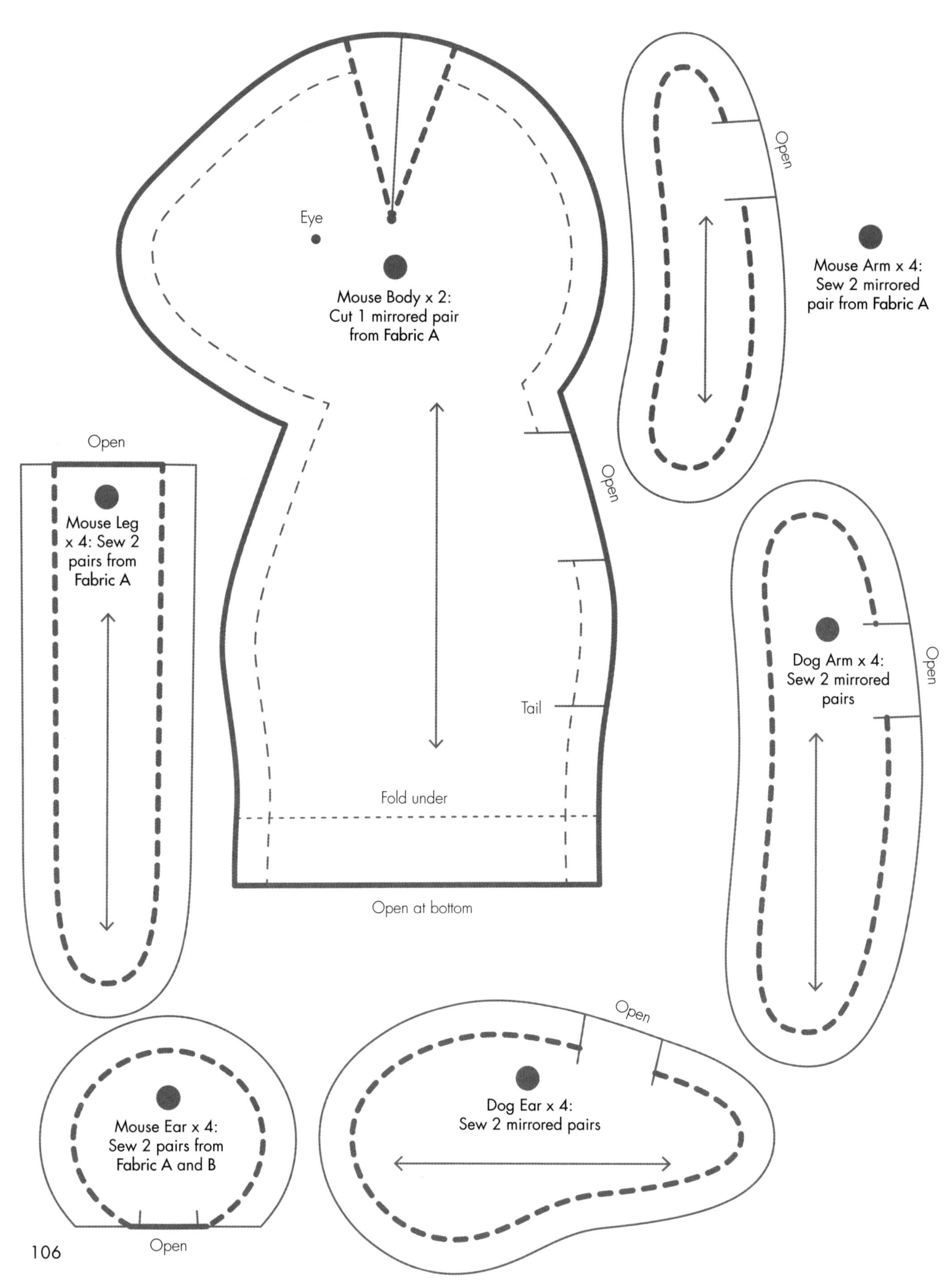
Eye
Mouse Body x 2:
Cut 1 mirrored pair
from Fabric A
Open
Tail
Fold under
Open at bottom
Open
Mouse Arm x 4:
Sew 2 mirrored
pair from Fabric A
Open
Mouse Leg
x 4: Sew 2
pairs from
Fabric A
Dog Arm x 4:
Sew 2 mirrored
pairs
Open
Open
Dog Ear x 4:
Sew 2 mirrored pairs
Mouse Ear x 4:
Sew 2 pairs from
Fabric A and B
Open

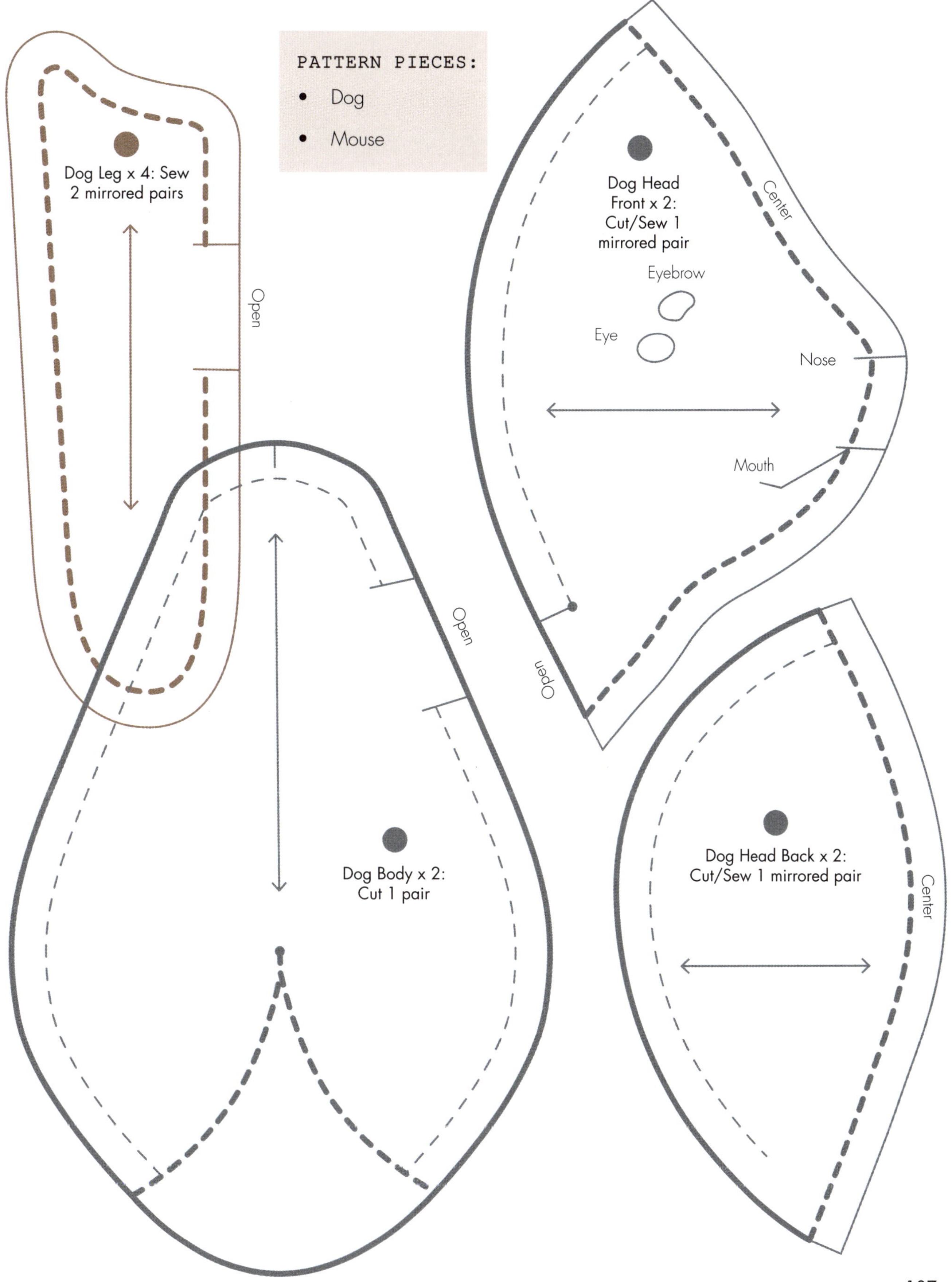
PATTERN PIECES:
• Dog
• Mouse
Dog Leg x 4: Sew
2 mirrored pairs
Open
Dog Head
Front x 2:
Cut/Sew 1
mirrored pair
Center
Eyebrow
Eye
Nose
Mouth
Open
Open
Dog Body x 2:
Cut 1 pair
Dog Head Back x 2:
Cut/Sew 1 mirrored pair
Center

projects

SECTION THREE

In Section 3 we're exploring gussets, yet another means to add roundness and dimensionality to our dolls. We'll sew a darling Bunny Rabbit and revisit two animals from Section 1, a Cat and a Bear. However, this time around we'll be using gussets and a combination of the new construction methods we've been learning along the way. How far we've come!

cat

This doll was inspired by my kitty boy Ernest and his striped tummy. If you're ever in need of a sleepy cat to warm your lap, he's your guy! We begin our exploration of gussets with a simple triangular gusset. The construction of the cat's head is similar to that of the Fox – one back piece, two front pieces – with the addition of a gusset inserted between the front pieces.

SKILL LEVEL: ADVANCED BEGINNER

FINISHED SIZE: 13IN (33CM)

MATERIALS AND SPECIAL TOOLS FOR CAT

- Pattern pieces (see pages 15 and 132–133)
- **Fabric A**, medium-weight cotton or linen/cotton blend: 30 x 6½in (76 x 16.5cm)
    - Head Front x 2: Cut 1 mirrored pair
    - Head Gusset x 1: Cut 1
    - Head Back x 1: Cut 1
    - Arm x 4: Sew 2 mirrored pairs
    - Leg x 4: Sew 2 mirrored pairs
    - Ear x 4: Sew 2 mirrored pairs
- **Fabric B**, medium-weight cotton or linen/cotton blend: 10½ x 5¾in (26.5 x 14.5cm)
    - Body Front x 2: Cut 1 mirrored pair
    - Body Back x 1: Cut 1
- Doll needle and strong thread to attach arms
- Embroidery Floss in pink and black
- Powder blush, beeswax crayon, colored pencil, or pink felt for cheeks (optional)

GUSSETS

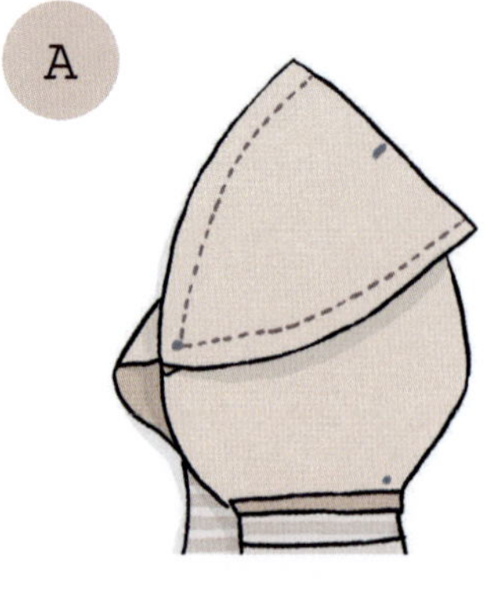

A gusset is a piece of fabric, usually triangular or seed-shaped, which is inserted in a seam in order to provide width and dimensionality. Like darts, they take a flat shape and transform it into a three-dimensional form. In doll-making, you will typically see gussets used on the head, inserted between two pieces from the nose to the top of the forehead (triangular gusset, see A, right) or from the nose to the back of the head where it meets the neck (seed-shaped gusset, see B, right). They function to give the head a rounded form and can be used to shape a muzzle. The process for sewing the gusset is a bit different for each of the dolls in this section, providing an opportunity for you to gain some experience sewing a range of gusset styles.

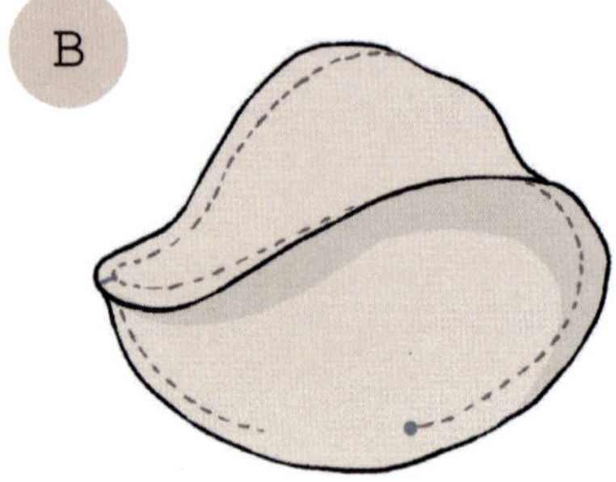

A gusset can be wide or narrow, short or long, but regardless of its shape, two factors are vital. First, the gusset must be symmetrical from side to side. When cutting out a gusset pattern piece or designing a gusset, keep the pattern piece folded in half to ensure that both sides of the gusset will be symmetrical. Second, the gusset must be inserted evenly between two pieces (usually head pieces) so that the seams begin and end at the same spot on both pieces. With a triangular gusset, the end points don't meet but they are placed in the same location on both head pieces. In the example of the seed-shaped gusset, you can see that the gusset begins at the tip of the nose and ends at the bottom of the head. The dot at the bottom of the piece shows where the gusset ends and the head pieces meet.

Designing with gussets is one of the most challenging aspects of doll-designing and more complicated than can be covered here. My best advice for now is for you to gain experience sewing a variety of patterns with gussets. Next, try modifying the shape of the gusset on a few existing patterns to study how this affects the shape of the head. In this way, you will have an understanding of how gussets work before moving on to designing.

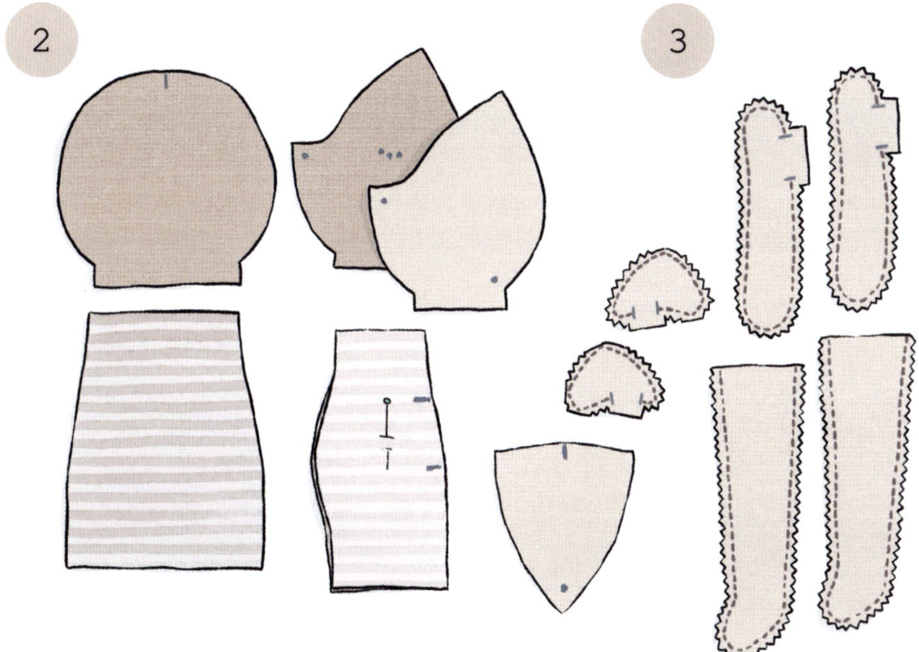

1. ***Transfer patterns and markings for all pieces as follows***. Take note of which fabric you'll be using for each piece and take care to transfer the correct lines as indicated: either the stitch line (without seam allowance) or the cutting line (with seam allowance included). When transferring stitch lines, be sure to leave ample space around the pattern pieces.

   On a 22 x 6½in (56 x 16.5cm) piece of **Fabric A** which has been folded in half with right sides together so that you will have mirrored pieces, transfer Head Front pattern on cutting line. Once cut, transfer face detail markings to right sides of fabric and neck pivot markings to wrong sides of fabric. Transfer marking for gusset start point to wrong side of top piece and right side of bottom piece.

   Transfer Arm, Leg and Ear patterns twice each on stitch line. The top of the Leg remains open. For Arms and Ears, transfer markings for opening to wrong side of fabric.

   On a 7¾ x 5in (19.5 x 13cm) piece of **Fabric A**, transfer Head Gusset on cutting line. Transfer markings to wrong side of fabric. Transfer Head Back pattern on cutting line. Transfer top center marking to right side of fabric.

   On a 6 x 5¾in (15 x 14.5cm) piece of **Fabric B** which has been folded in half with right sides together so that you will have mirrored pieces, transfer Body Front pattern on cutting line. Transfer marking for opening to wrong side of fabric.

   On a 4½ x 5¾in (11.5 x 14.5cm) piece of **Fabric B**, transfer Body Back pattern on cutting line.

2. Cut out all pieces for which you transferred cutting lines.

3. ***Sew all pieces for which you transferred stitch lines – Arms, Legs and Ears***. Sew directly on stitch line, leaving openings as marked. Cut out around the sewing line with pinking shears. For Ears, trim seam allowance carefully to reduce bulk and get nice corners; clip off corner points at a diagonal and trim seam allowance very close to the stitching line leading up to the corners. Turn all pieces right side out and press out seams.

CONTINUES...

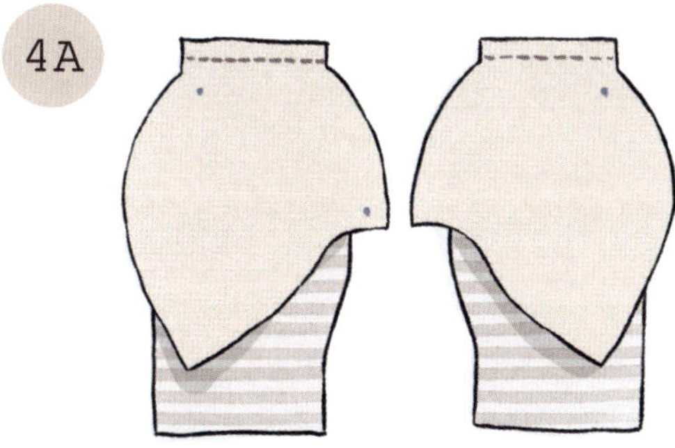

4. *Lay Head Front pieces over Body Front pieces* with right sides together, making sure that you have correctly paired left and right sides. Sew along neck edge (see 4A). Press open seams. These are now called Front pieces. Lay Head Back piece over Body Back piece with right sides together. Sew along neck edge (see 4B). Press open seam. This is now called the Back piece.

5. With right sides facing, match up the gusset start points on one Front piece and on Gusset piece and pin to hold. The edges should align at the tip. Next, match up the other end of the seam (at forehead) and pin to secure.

   Continue aligning edges and pinning while easing the Gusset around the curve of the Front piece. Use lots of pins. Push any wrinkles that form away from the edge, pinning them out of the way if need be.

6. To begin sewing, manually lower the needle on your machine so that the first stitch begins exactly at the gusset start point. Be sure to anchor your seam well, but take care not to backstitch past the dot. Sew from gusset start point to forehead.

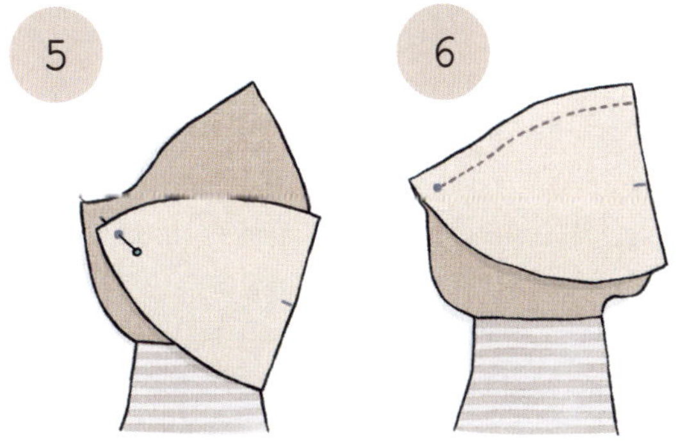

7. Repeat for the other side of the Gusset. Fold back the tip of the nose on the first Front piece so that it doesn't get caught in the seam for the second side. It may help to pin it out of the way. Note, because you will be sewing from the tip of the nose to the forehead for both pieces, you will sew with the Gusset piece on top for one side and the Front piece on top for the other side. Do not trim the seam allowance yet.

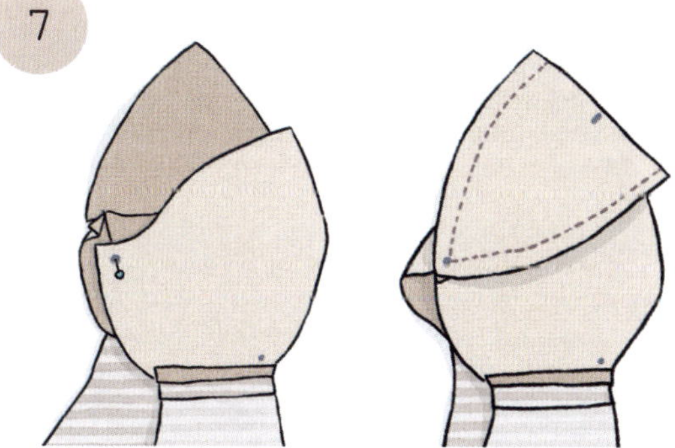

CONTINUES...

8. *Fold the Gusset piece* neatly along its center so that the two Front pieces are evenly aligned with right sides facing. Starting at the gusset start point, sew the Front pieces together right down to the bottom edge. Reinforce the seam at the throat with an extra row of stitching.

Clip off the seam allowance at the tip of the nose, taking care not to cut through any stitch lines. Clip curves and trim seam allowances with pinking shears. Press open seams, using your fingers to press them open if you can't get your iron into the rounded seams.

9. *Pin Front to Back* – Lay the Front piece over the Back piece. Align at top center markings and at neck seam. Take care that the gusset seams are fully pressed open as you pin around the top of the head.

10. Sew around from bottom edge to bottom edge, pausing at neck markings with the needle in the down position in order to pivot the fabric. Leave an opening at the side as marked. The bottom is not sewn. Reinforce the seams at the neck with an extra row of stitching. Clip curves, trim seam allowance and clip into the neck corners. Turn right side out and press out seams.

11. Turn the bottom edge under ½in (1.2cm) to the inside all the way round and press well to get a crisp crease. You can use a ruler and disappearing-ink pen if you'd like to draw a line ½in (1.2cm) up from the bottom edge of the Body on each side to ensure a straight and even fold.

12. Stuff the head firmly until just past the neck.

13. *Add the Legs* – Stuff Legs to about ¾in (2cm) from top. At the opening, line up the two seams so that they meet and so that the foot is now pointing forward. Press and pin or baste to maintain alignment and to hold the stuffing in place. Repeat for second Leg.

14. Insert Legs through the bottom opening of the Body so that the top ½in (1.2cm) of each Leg is sandwiched inside. Position the Legs as far towards the sides of the Body as possible and be sure the toes are pointing forward. Pin or baste to hold. Sew right along the bottom edge ⅛in (3mm) in from the edge. Run an additional line of stitching on top of the first to ensure strength of seam. Remove basting stitches, if necessary.

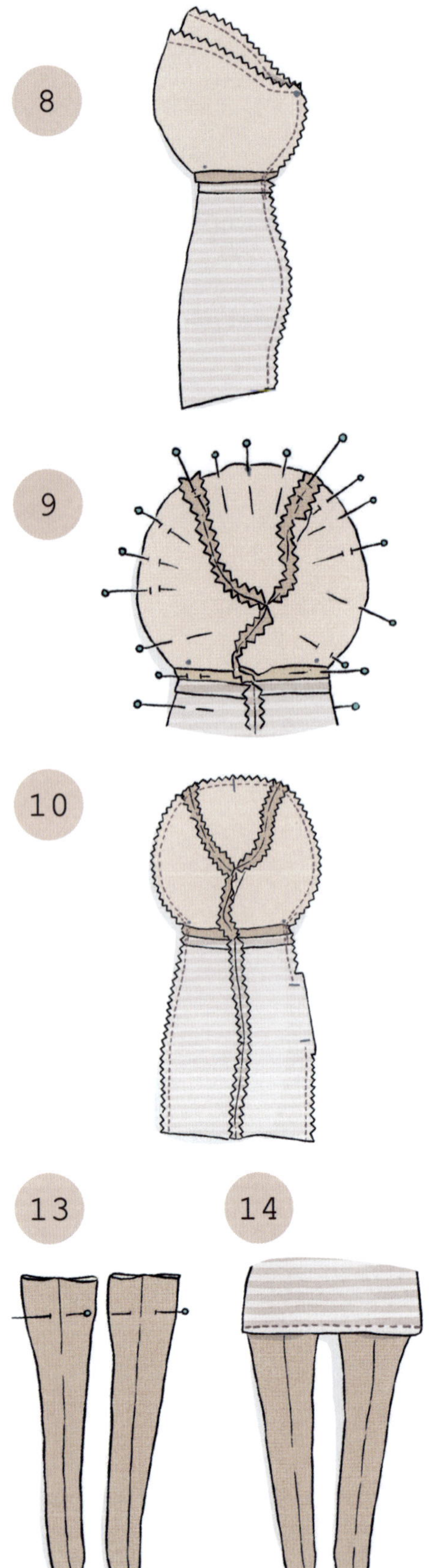

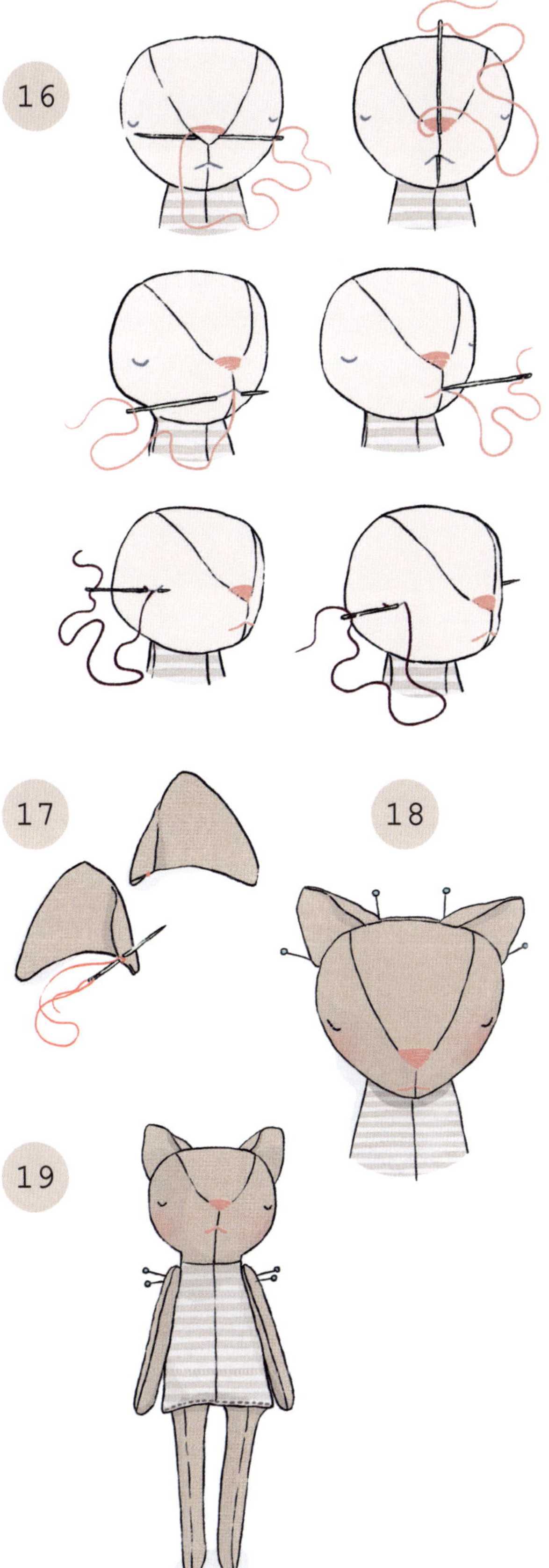

15. Continue stuffing the Body through the side opening until packed firmly, then close with ladder stitch.

16. *Embroider face details* – See Embroidery Stitches on pages 29–30. First, draw in the face details with disappearing-ink pen. With pink embroidery floss, use satin stitch to create the nose. With the same length of floss, make two straight stitches for the mouth. For closed eyes, use backstitch in black embroidery floss. For open eyes, draw with fabric marker or embroider using satin stitch.

17. *Ears* – Use ladder stitch to close openings. Fold Ears as indicated on pattern, making sure that the two Ears are mirrored. Secure fold with a small hand-sewn stitch at the bottom edge.

18. Position Ears along seam and pin in place. The folded side of the Ear is towards the center and positioned about ½in (1.2cm) from the gusset seam. Attach with ladder stitch (see page 86).

19. *Add the Arms* – First, stuff Arms and ladder stitch closed. Position Arms at side seam about ¼in (6mm) down from neck seam and attach (see pages 26–27).

bunny rabbit

This lovely, long-eared and long-limbed Bunny Rabbit is a relatively simple design, but packed with charm. It's constructed with two side pieces and a gusset that starts at the nose, narrows at the neck and then extends all the way down, becoming the back body piece. I like Bunny dolls with ears that stand up straight so I add an extra layer of batting or soft fabric inside the ears. For a floppier look, forgo the batting layer and choose a lighter-weight fabric for the inner ear. Use a mix of fabrics for ears and limbs or use the same fabric throughout.

SKILL LEVEL: CONFIDENT BEGINNER

FINISHED SIZE: 15½IN (39.5CM) WITH TALL EARS, 12½IN (32CM) WITH FLOPPY EARS

MATERIALS AND SPECIAL TOOLS FOR RABBIT

- Pattern pieces (see pages 15 and 133–134)
- **Fabric A**, medium-weight cotton or linen/cotton blend: 14¼ x 13¼in (36 x 33.5cm)
  - Side x 2: Cut 1 mirrored pair
  - Gusset x 1: Cut 1
  - Ear x 2: Sew 2 mirrored pairs from **Fabric A** and **C**
- **Fabric B**, medium-weight cotton or linen/cotton blend: 16½ x 7in (42 x 18cm)
  - Arm x 4: Sew 2 mirrored pairs
  - Leg x 4: Sew 2 mirrored pairs
- **Fabric C**, medium-weight cotton or linen/cotton blend, or light-weight cotton or linen for floppy ears: 5¼ x 4¾in (13.5 x 12cm)
  - Ear x 2: Sew 2 mirrored pairs from **Fabric A** and **C**
- Embroidery Floss in pink
- Black gel fabric marker (optional)
- Doll needle
- Powder blush, beeswax crayon, colored pencil, or pink felt for cheeks (optional)

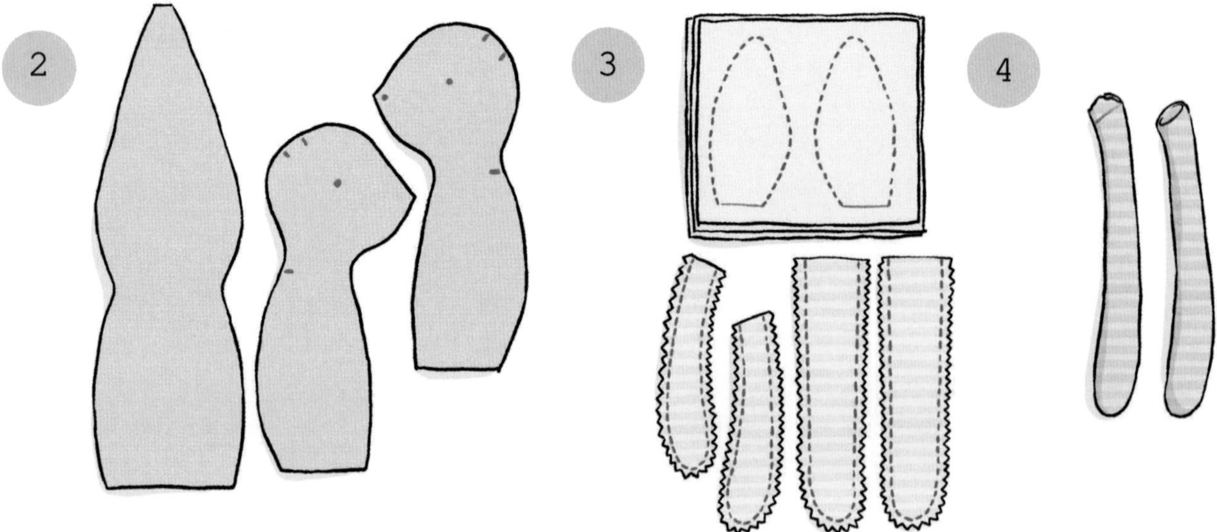

1. ***Transfer patterns and markings for all pieces as follows.*** Take note of which fabric you'll be using for each piece and take care to transfer the correct lines as indicated: either the stitch line (without seam allowance) or the cutting line (with seam allowance included). When transferring stitch lines, be sure to leave ample space around the pattern pieces.

On a 9 x 9in (23 x 23cm) piece of **Fabric A** which has been folded in half with right sides together so that you will have mirrored pieces, transfer Side pattern on cutting line, taking note of the grainline. Once cut, transfer Eye, Ear and Arm placement markings to right sides of both pieces. Transfer markings for opening placement to wrong side of top piece. Transfer marking for gusset start point to right side of top piece and wrong side of bottom piece.

On a 12¼ x 4¼in (31 x 11cm) piece of **Fabric A,** transfer Gusset pattern on cutting line taking note of the grainline. Transfer gusset start point, Arm placement markings and marking at center of bottom edge to wrong side of fabric.

On the 16½ x 7in (42 x 18cm) piece of **Fabric B** which has been folded in half with right sides together so that you will have mirrored pieces, transfer Arm and Leg patterns twice each on stitch line. Arms and Legs remain open at the top for turning and stuffing.

Cut a 5¼ x 4¾in (13.5 x 12cm) piece each of **Fabrics A, C** and optional batting layer. Lay **A** over **C** with right sides together. If using a batting layer, place it underneath **Fabrics A** and **C**, at the bottom of the stack. Transfer Ear pattern twice on stitch line, flipping over the pattern piece for the second Ear so that you will have a mirrored set. The bottom edge is left open for turning.

2. Cut out Side and Gusset pieces.

3. ***Sew Arms, Legs and Ears*** – Sew directly on stitch line, leaving openings at tops of Arms and Legs and at base of Ears. Cut out around the sewing line with pinking shears (see page 22). Turn right side out and press out seams, paying special attention to the tips of the Ears.

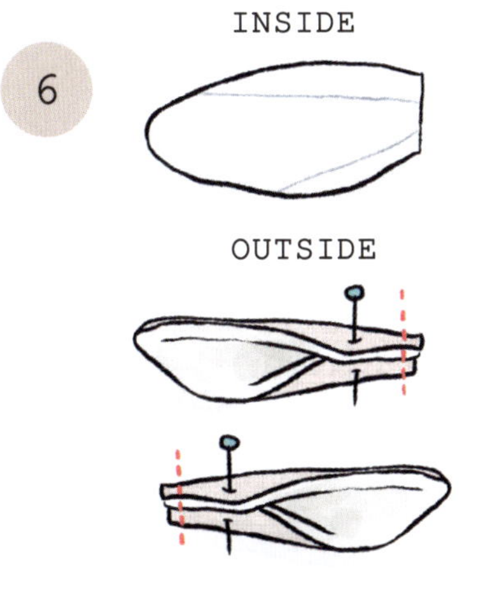

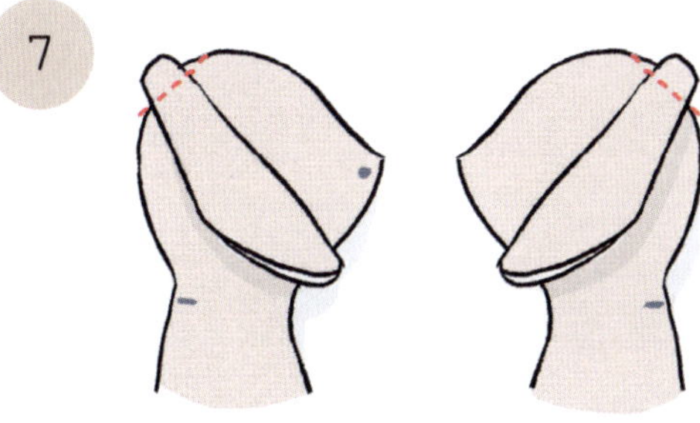

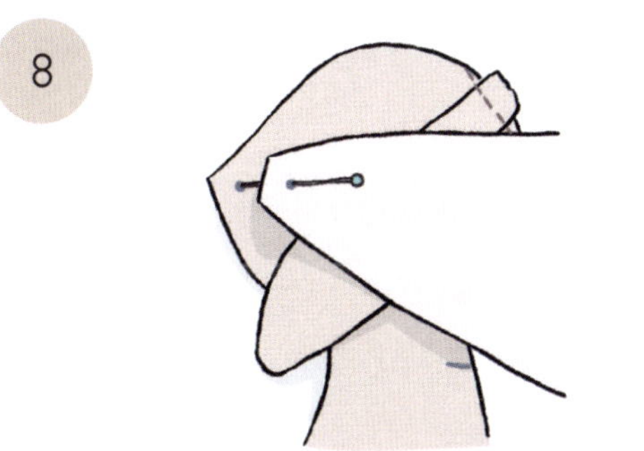

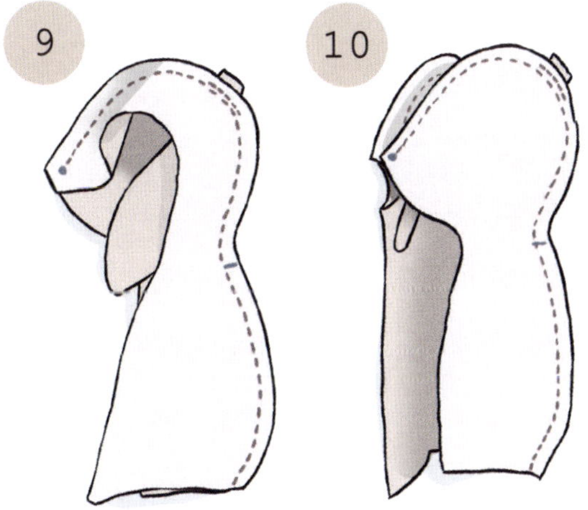

4. Stuff Arms to about ¾in (2cm) from top. Clip off triangle at top of Arm as marked on pattern, then turn seam under ¼in (6mm) to the inside all the way around and press well to get a crisp crease. If you'd like, you can use a ruler and disappearing-ink pen to draw a line ¼in (6mm) down from the top edge of the Arm on each side to ensure a straight and even fold.

5. Stuff Legs to about ¾in (2cm) from top.

6. *Fold Ears* – Fold the outside edge in first, then fold the inside edge over top. Baste along the base of Ears to hold.

7. *Baste Ears to Side pieces* – Position Ears on Side pieces with right sides facing/**Fabric C** facing down. The inside fold should be closer to the nose and the outside fold further from the nose. The base of the Ears should overlap the top of the Side piece by about ⅛in (3mm). Be sure that both Ears are positioned at the same angle, as marked on pattern. Baste along edge to hold in place.

8. *Pin Gusset to first Side piece* – With right sides facing, match up the gusset start points on one Side piece and on Gusset piece, and pin to hold. The edges should align at the tip. Next, match up Arm markings on Side and Gusset pieces and pin. Starting back at the nose, continue aligning edges and pinning while easing the Gusset around the curve of the Side piece. Use lots of pins! Push any wrinkles that form away from the edge, pinning them out of the way if need be. Continue pinning to bottom edge. *Optional* – baste by hand to hold in place.

9. *Sew Gusset to first Side piece* – To begin sewing, manually lower the needle on your machine so that the first stitch begins exactly at the gusset start point. Secure the seam well, but don't backstitch past the gusset start point. Sew to bottom edge. Reinforce seam at Ear with a second row of stitching.

10. Repeat steps 8 and 9 for the second Side piece. Fold back the tip of the nose on the first side piece so that it doesn't get caught in the seam for the second Side piece. Pin it out of the way if need be. Take note – because you will be sewing from the tip of the nose towards the back of the head for both pieces, you will sew with the Gusset piece on top for the first side and with the Side piece on top for the second side.

CONTINUES...

11. Trim seam allowances from the bottom edge to just below the ear on both sides with pinking shears. Press open seams to just above arm markings.

12. The attachment method we'll use for the arms is a bit more involved than attaching them after the doll has been stuffed and closed, but because it's machine sewn, it's much more secure. Arms are sewn to the outside of the doll/right side of the fabric. Turn the piece right side out and position Arms at Arm markings so that they are centered over the seam, facing forward and positioned at the same angle. Pin Arms in place. Check the wrong side to be sure that the seam allowances are fully open and laying flat.

13. ***Attach Arms*** – Lay the piece as open and flat as you can. Sew two rows of stitching parallel to the top edge of the Arm, the first as close to the edge as possible and the second ¼in (6mm) down from the edge. Sew back and forth several times on each row to make a strong attachment, but take care not to stitch past the Arm and directly into the Body. Repeat for second Arm.

14. ***Sew Side pieces together*** – Turn the piece wrong side out and align Side pieces carefully with right sides together. Fold the gusset up along its center and tuck arms and ears out of the way. Sew from the gusset start point to bottom edge, leaving an opening as marked. Reinforce the seam at the throat with an extra row of stitching. Clip off seam allowance at the tip of the nose. Clip curves and trim seam allowance with pinking shears, leaving uncut tab at opening. Trim seam allowance on both sides of the head from the nose to just before the ear. Do not trim seam allowance above the ears. Turn right side out and press out seams, taking care to push out the nose completely.

15. At bottom edge, align the center seam on the front with the marking on the back piece. Turn the bottom edge of the Body under ½in (1.2cm) to the inside and press well to get a crisp crease. You can use a ruler and disappearing-ink pen to draw a line ½in (1.2cm) up from the bottom edge of the Body on each side to ensure a straight and even fold.

16. Stuff the head firmly through the bottom opening. Stuff until just past the neck.

13A

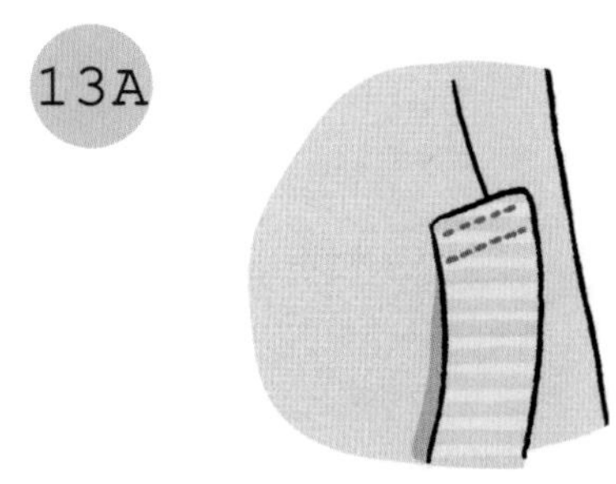

13B

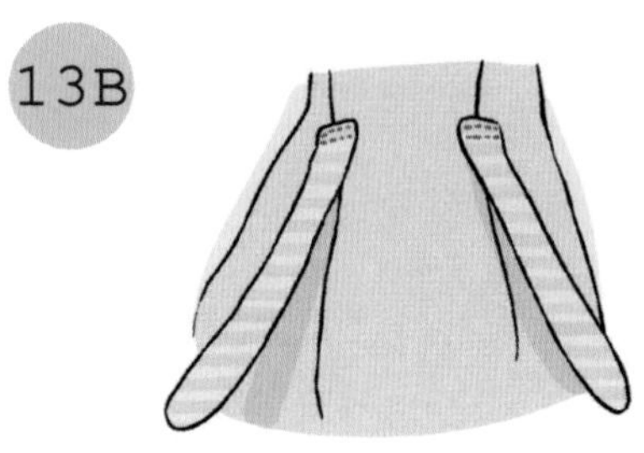

14

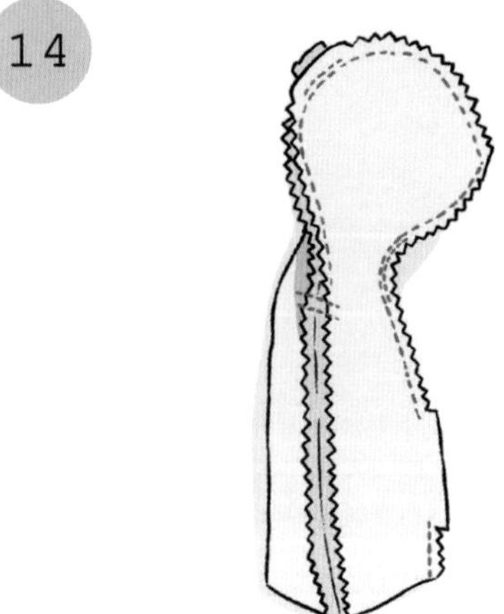

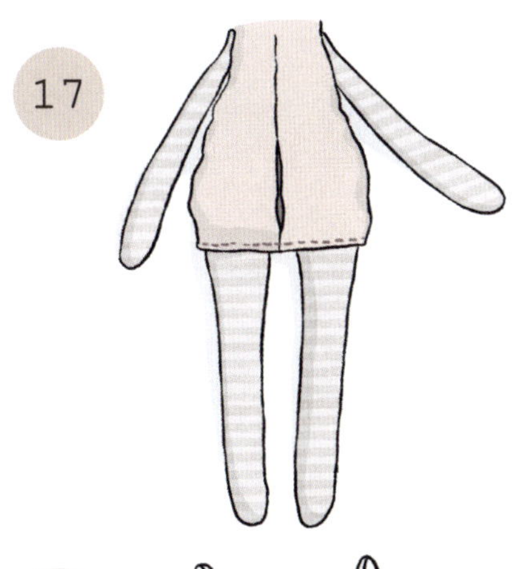

17. ***Attach Legs*** – Insert Legs so that the top ½in (1.2cm) of each Leg is sandwiched inside the Body. Position them as far towards the sides of the Body as possible and be sure the toes are pointing inward. Pin or baste in place. Sew right along the bottom edge ⅛in (3mm) from the edge. Run a second line of stitching over the first to ensure strength of seam. Remove basting stitches if necessary.

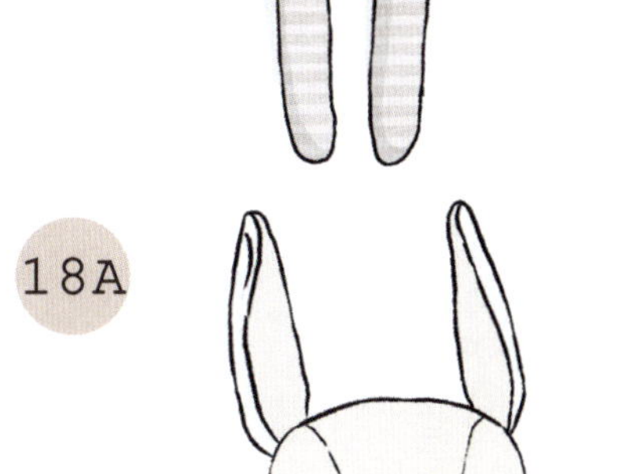

18. ***Embroider face details*** – see Embroidery Stitches on pages 29–30. Using 3-strands of pink embroidery floss, embroider the nose with satin stitch and the mouth with two straight stitches. Tie off knot under an arm or inside an ear. Embroider the eyes or draw them in with black fabric marker.

19. Stuff the Body through the center seam until packed firmly, then close with ladder stitch (see page 25).

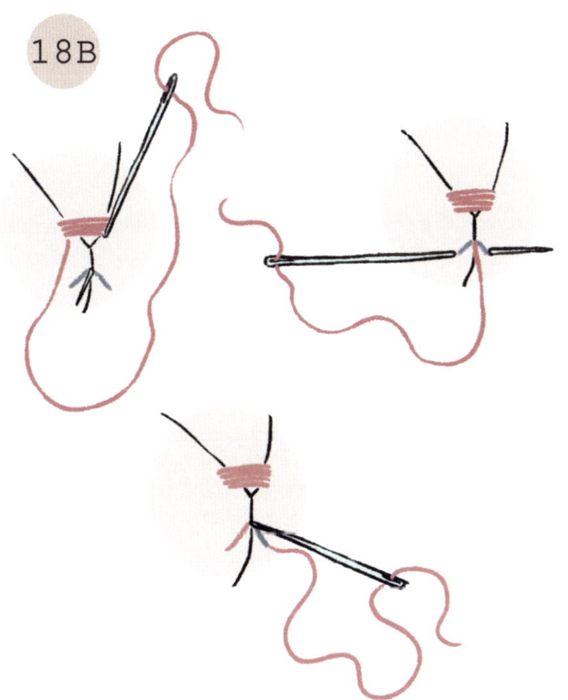

This doll is dedicated to my papa whose name is Björn: bear in Swedish. When he moved to the US, he went by the name Ted or Teddy. He was noble, kind and gentle, as teddy bears should be. Our final project incorporates many of the construction methods and elements we've practiced throughout this book. It may seem a bit complex but don't be daunted! Just take your time, following the steps carefully.

SKILL LEVEL: ADVANCED

FINISHED SIZE: 11IN (28CM)

MATERIALS AND SPECIAL TOOLS FOR BEAR

- Pattern pieces (see pages 15 and 133–135)
- **Fabric A**, medium-weight cotton or linen/cotton blend: 34 x 7½in (86.5 x 19cm)
    - – Head x 2: Cut 1 mirrored pair
    - – Gusset x 1: Cut 1
    - – Body Front x 2: Cut 1 mirrored pair
    - – Body Back x 2: Cut 1 mirrored pair
    - – Ear x 2: Cut 1 pair
    - – Arm x 4: Sew 2 mirrored pairs
    - – Leg x 4: Sew 2 mirrored pairs
- **Fabric B**, medium-weight cotton or linen/cotton blend: 6 x 2in (15 x 5cm)
    - – Ear x 2: Cut 1 pair
- Doll needle and strong thread to attach arms
- Embroidery floss in black and white, and in brown (optional) for the nose and mouth
- Powder blush, beeswax crayon, colored pencil, or pink felt for cheeks (optional)

EMBROIDERED BEAR NOSE

The nose on a Bear will help determine their look and personality. An embroidered nose is made with satin stitch, regardless of its shape or size. The smaller and simpler the nose, the easier it will be to get good results as it will require fewer stitches. The nose for this Bear is positioned just at the end of the gusset and made with horizontal satin stitch. For the experienced or courageous embroiderer, there are a variety of shapes and sizes to experiment with.

Begin by drawing the outline of the nose shape on your Bear with disappearing-ink pen. You may choose to use a permanent marker in the same color as your embroidery floss to outline or fill in the shape; this helps to camouflage any spots where the stitching is not perfectly lined up, but be sure to test the marker on scrap fabric first to be sure it doesn't bleed!

- *Horizontal satin-stitch nose* – Where you begin stitching depends on which shape of nose you are making. Because our nose begins just across the end of the gusset, we start at the top corner of the nose with the first stitch laying over the curved seam of the gusset. Continue to make horizontal stitches, doing your best to keep the side edges even. Fill in the nose from top to bottom.

- *Triangle nose* – A triangle nose is relatively beginner friendly and a good option if you'd like the nose to straddle the area above and below the gusset seam. Bring the needle up at 1, centered at the top of the nose. Reinsert at 2 into the bottom point of the triangle, using the chin seam as a guide to ensure the stitch is centered. Bring the needle back up at 3 just next to 1. For each subsequent stitch alternate left and right along the top edge of the nose, each time reinserting at 2 into the same spot at the bottom point of the triangle.

- *Vertical satin-stitch nose* – Follow the directions for the triangle nose, starting at the top center of the nose and alternating stitches from side to side, but using straight vertical stitches, as shown.

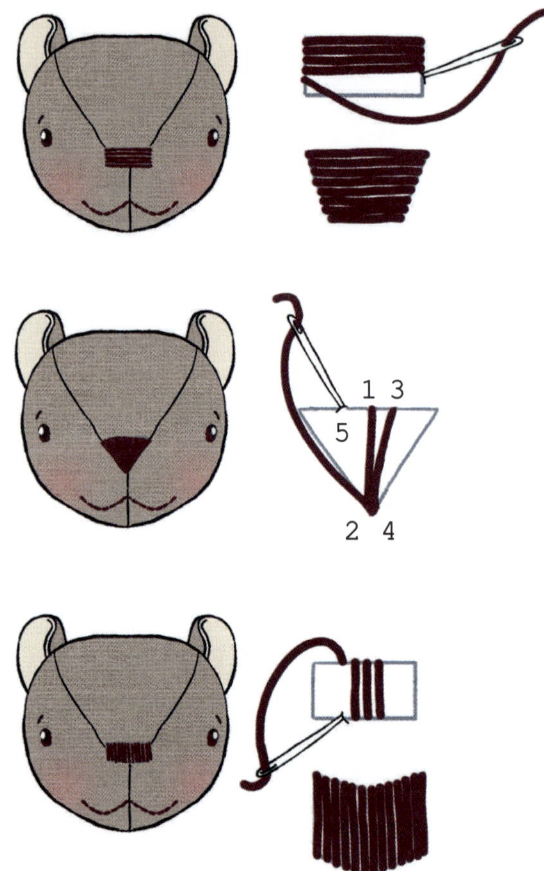

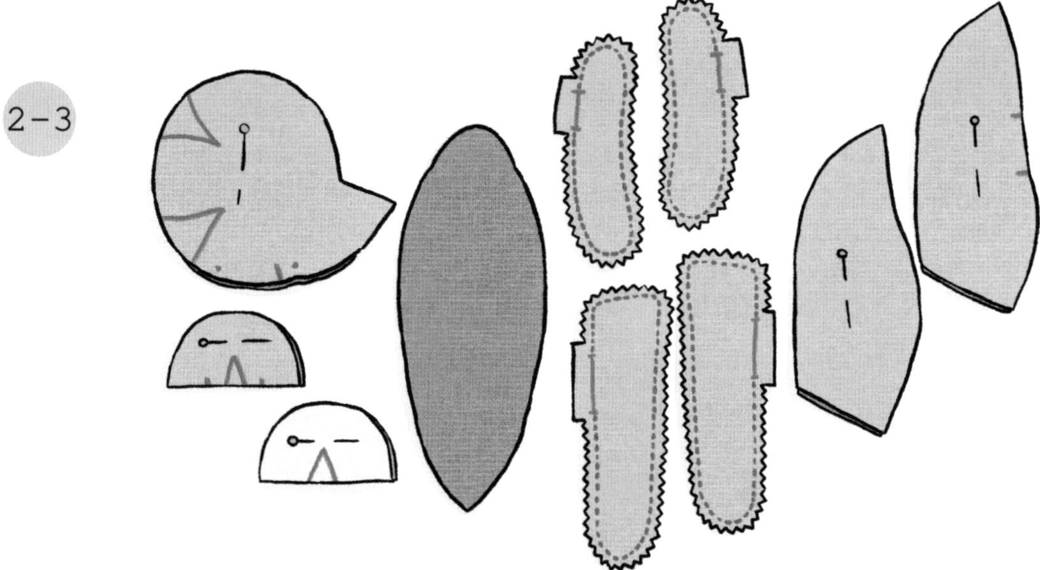

1. *Transfer patterns and markings for all pieces as follows*. Take care to transfer the correct lines as indicated: either the stitch line (without seam allowance) or the cutting line (with seam allowance included). When transferring stitch lines, be sure to leave ample space around the pattern pieces.

On a 30½ x 6¼in (77.5 x 16cm) piece of **Fabric A** which has been folded in half with right sides together so that you will have mirrored pieces, transfer Head pattern on cutting line, taking note of the grainline. Once cut, transfer A, C, pivot and dart markings to wrong sides of fabric. Transfer eye and B markings to right sides of fabric. Transfer Body Front and Body Back patterns on cutting line. Transfer markings for opening to Body Back. Transfer Arm and Leg patterns twice each on stitch line. Transfer markings for openings. Transfer Ear pattern on cutting line. Transfer the markings for darts and openings to wrong sides.

On a 3½ x 7½in (9 x 19cm) piece of **Fabric A**, transfer Gusset pattern on cutting line. Transfer all markings to wrong side of fabric.

On a 6 x 2in (15 x 5cm) piece of **Fabric B** which has been folded in half with right sides together so that you will have mirrored pieces, transfer Ear pattern on cutting line. Once cut, transfer dart markings to wrong sides of fabric.

2. Cut out all the pieces for which you transferred cutting lines.

3. *Sew all pieces for which you transferred stitch lines* – Arms and Legs. Sew directly on stitch line, leaving openings as marked. Cut out around the sewing line with pinking shears. Turn all pieces right side out and press out seams. Stuff Arms and Legs and ladder stitch closed (see page 25).

4. Sew Body Front pieces with right sides together along center seam. Sew Body Back pieces with right sides together along center seam, leaving opening for stuffing. Clip curves/trim seam allowance with zigzag scissors and press open the seams.

CONTINUES...

5. Lay Body Back over Body Front with right sides facing, aligning center seams at top and bottom. Sew all the way around. Clip curves/trim seams with pinking shears. Turn right side out and press out seams. Stuff firmly and ladder stitch closed.

6. *Make Ears* – Sew darts on all four Ear pieces. Lay each **Fabric A** Ear over a **Fabric B** Ear with right sides facing. Sew around leaving opening for turning. Clip corners and curves and trim seams with pinking shears, leaving uncut tabs at openings. Turn right side out and press out seams. Close with ladder stitch.

7. ***Sew darts on Gusset and Head pieces.*** For all darts, press seam allowance away from nose.

8. With right sides facing, sew Head pieces together along the chin seam from the top edge of the nose to A, pausing at the pivot marking with the needle in the down position to shift the fabric around. Clip seam allowance at tip of nose at an angle. Clip curves and trim seams with pinking shears, taking care to only trim the area that has been sewn. Press open seams.

9. With right sides facing, carefully match up nose marking on Gusset with the chin seam of the Head pieces, being sure that the seam allowance is pressed fully open. Pin directly through the center seam or secure with an anchoring stitch. Match up B markings on Gusset and Head pieces. Carefully angle the sides of the Gusset so that the markings are aligned.

   Pin from B markings to Gusset dart seams along both sides. The edges should line up perfectly. Now, ease the Gusset into the area between nose and B markings. They should fit like spoons. Pin to secure. Check carefully, including from underneath, for wrinkles. If necessary, redistribute fabric or push wrinkles away from the edge, pinning them out of the way. This is the most challenging part so take your time and use lots of pins. You may prefer to baste by hand to hold in place.

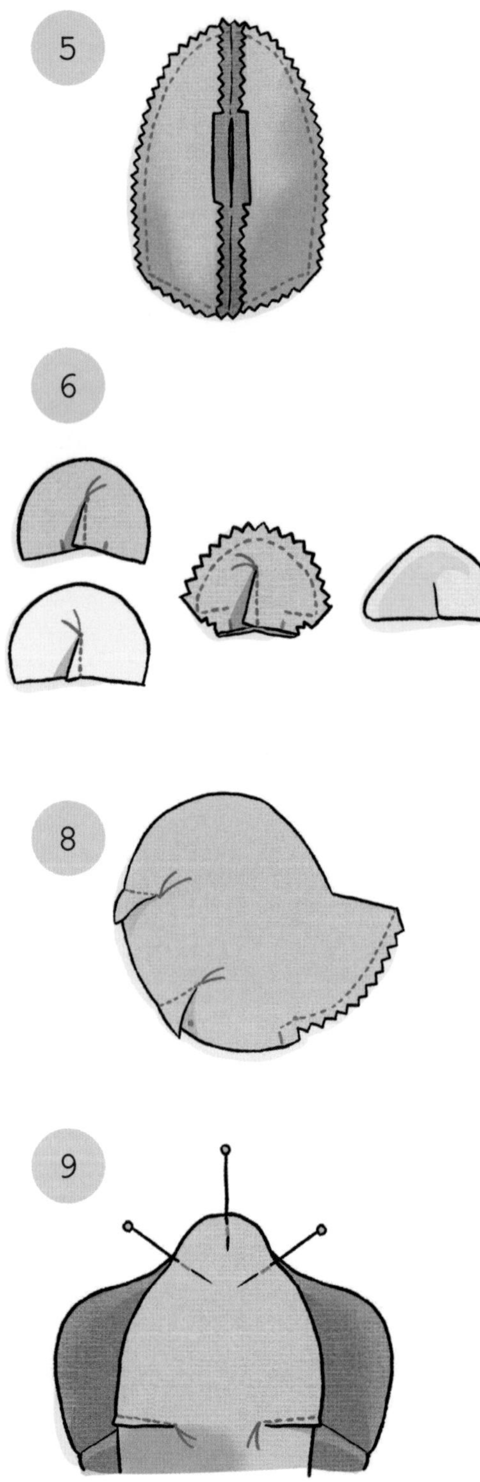

CONTINUES...

10. With the Gusset on top, sew from dart to dart along the area you've pinned, pivoting at the B markings to follow the edge of the fabric. Sew carefully around the nose, keeping an even seam allowance, as this will determine the shape of your Bear's muzzle. You may need to pause periodically, with the needle in the down position, to shift the fabric underneath to ensure it won't get sewn up into the seam

11. Without trimming the seam allowance, turn the work right side out and use your fingernail or a chopstick to push out the seam and look for any wrinkles or bumps. If you find any, that portion will need to be taken out with a seam ripper and restitched. No need to rip out the whole seam, just those few stitches. Readjust the fabric, re-pin and resew. It can help to gently pull the fabric towards you as you machine sew to create a bit more space to ease in the fabric. Check again for wrinkles or bumps.

12. Next, match up C markings on Gusset and one Head piece. Make sure all darts are pressed towards the back as you continue pinning the area from the Gusset dart to the C marking. Sew pinned area from front towards back. Repeat for the other side. Take note that on one side, the Gusset will be on top as you sew and for the other, the Head piece will be on top. Both sides should end exactly at the C marking. Leaving the seam allowance at the opening uncut, clip curves and trim seams with pinking shears. Turn right side out and press out seams. Tuck in seam allowance at opening and press well.

13. *Stuff the Head* – Begin by stuffing the nose area then continue stuffing the rest of the head, starting at the furthest area from the opening. Take care to stuff symmetrically, alternating side to side, so that your Bear's face will be even. Stuff filler into all the darts to help smooth out any points and create a nice shape. Pause now and then to look at the Head from various angles to make sure that it's even. Use your hands to mold the shape and feel for any empty areas. Once the rest of the Head is stuffed, add more filler to the muzzle area, packing the nose and chin firmly. Close the opening with ladder stitch (see page 25), beginning at the end closest to the muzzle and stitching towards the back.

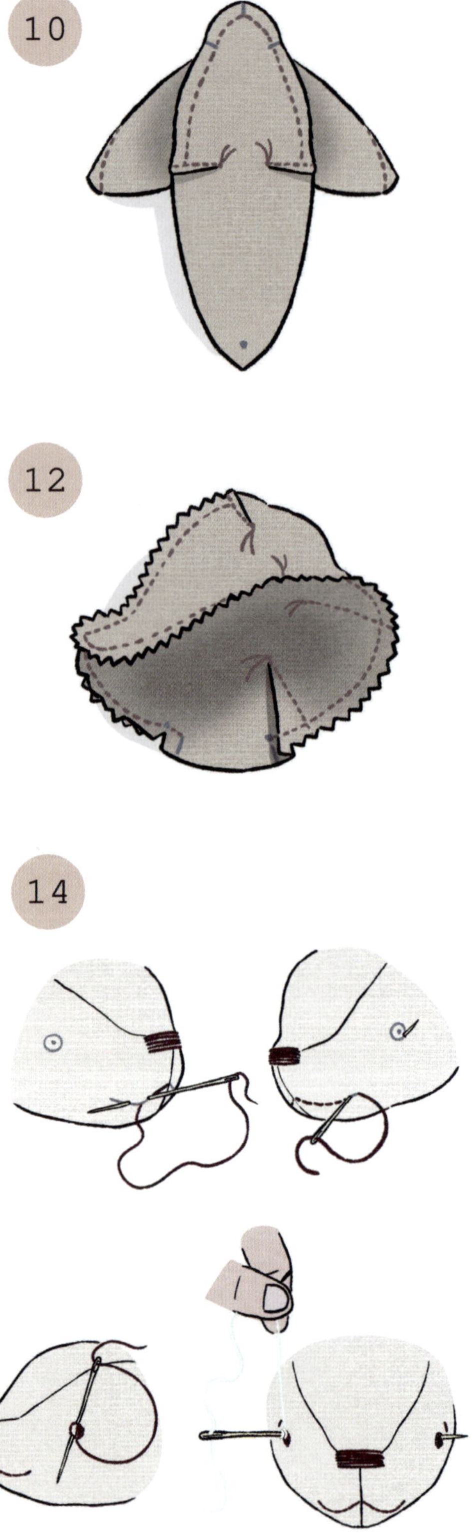

16B

16C

14. *Embroider the face details* – See Embroidery Stitches on pages 29–30. First, draw in details with disappearing-ink pen. Using 3 strands of black or brown embroidery floss, embroider the nose using satin stitch (see page 126). With the same length of floss, use backstitch to embroider the mouth starting approximately $\frac{5}{8}$in (1.5cm) below the gusset seam. With 3 strands of black embroidery floss, use backstitch to outline the eyes then fill in with satin stitch. Make a simple straight stitch for each of the eyebrows using 2 strands of black embroidery floss. With 3 strands of white embroidery floss, make a French knot or sew a few tiny straight stitches in each eye to create a highlight.

15. *Position the Head* with the ladder-stitched opening directly over the top of the Body, lining up seams at center front. Insert pins through the chest, angling them upwards into the Head to hold in place. Ladder stitch Head to Body, circling several times, each time increasing the circumference by stitching further up the Head and further down the Body (see page 100). Circle until the Head doesn't wobble when you shake the doll.

16. When positioning the Ears, consider how far forward/back or high/low they sit, as well as how curved they will be. Experiment with different positions, studying them from different angles. Pin Ears along front, back and center, then attach with ladder stitch (see page 86).

17. *Attach Arms and Legs* – Position the Arms $\frac{3}{8}$–$\frac{1}{2}$in (1–1.2cm) below the neck seam. Position Legs so that the outside edges line up with the edges of the Body. Attach Arms (see pages 26–27) and ladder stitch Legs to Body (see page 101).

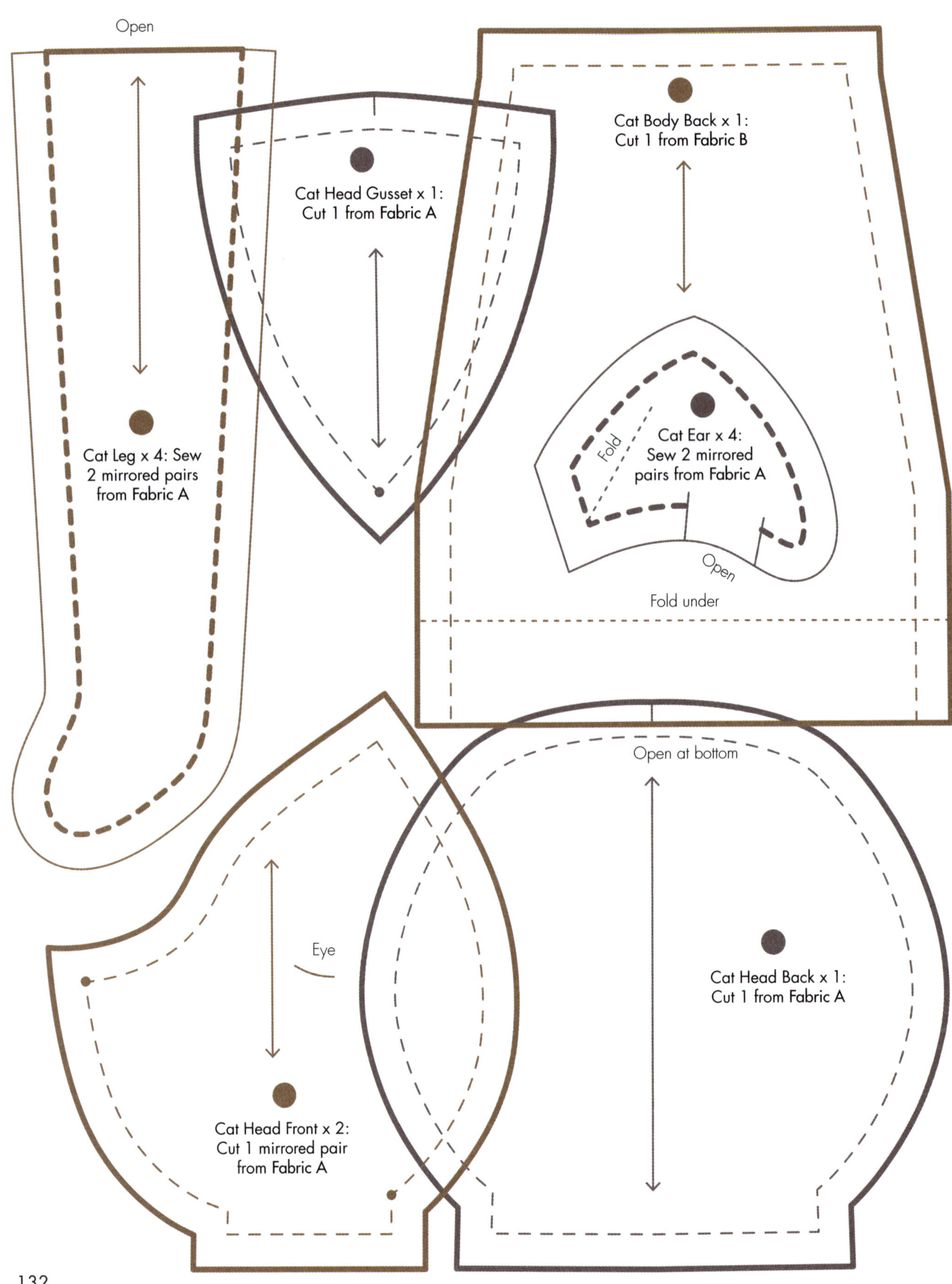
Open
Cat Leg x 4: Sew
2 mirrored pairs
from Fabric A
Cat Head Gusset x 1:
Cut 1 from Fabric A
Cat Body Back x 1:
Cut 1 from Fabric B
Fold
Cat Ear x 4:
Sew 2 mirrored
pairs from Fabric A
Open
Fold under
Open at bottom
Eye
Cat Head Front x 2:
Cut 1 mirrored pair
from Fabric A
Cat Head Back x 1:
Cut 1 from Fabric A

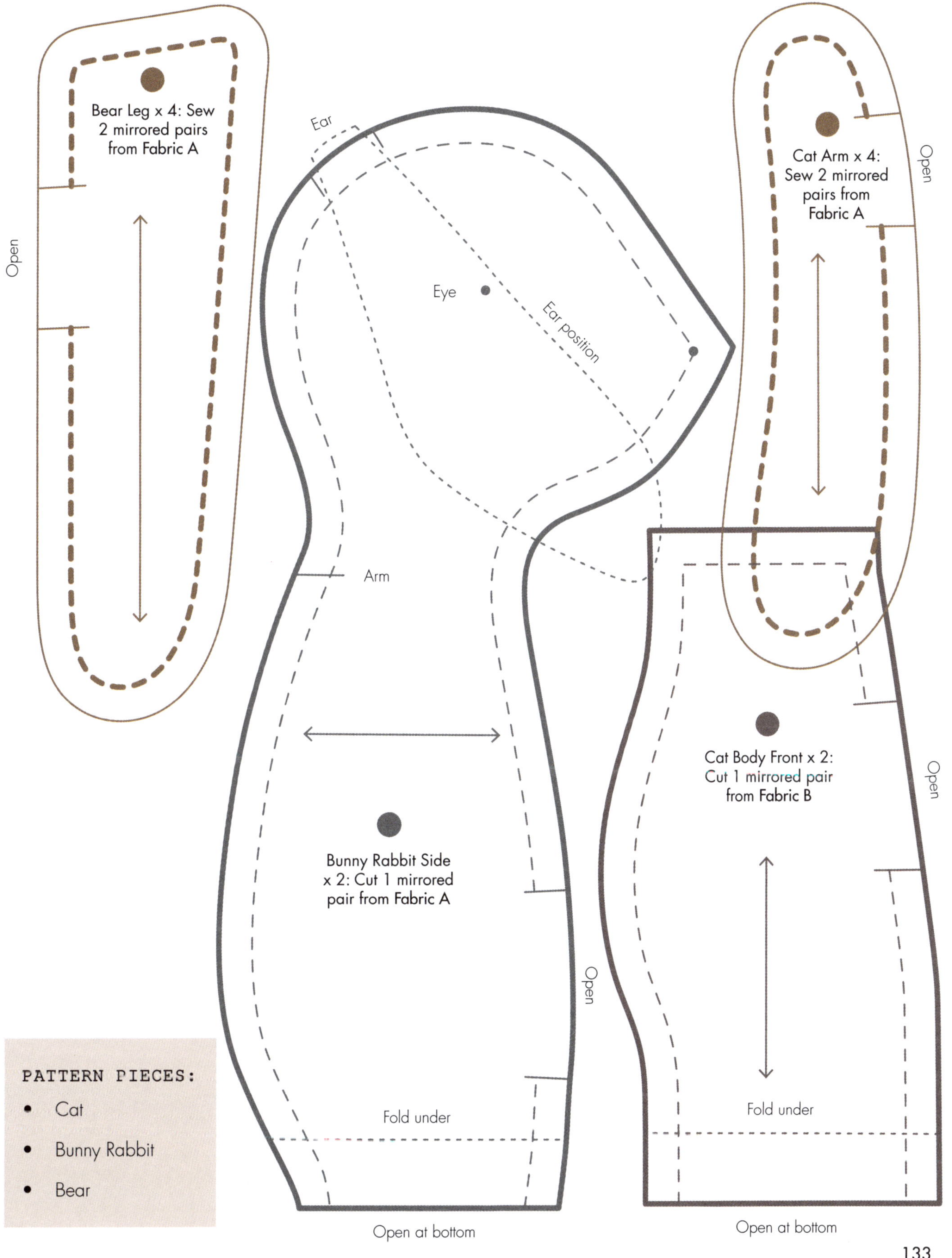
Bear Leg x 4: Sew 2 mirrored pairs from Fabric A
Open
Ear
Eye
Ear position
Arm
Bunny Rabbit Side x 2: Cut 1 mirrored pair from Fabric A
Open
Fold under
Open at bottom
Cat Arm x 4: Sew 2 mirrored pairs from Fabric A
Open
Cat Body Front x 2: Cut 1 mirrored pair from Fabric B
Open
Fold under
Open at bottom
PATTERN PIECES:
• Cat
• Bunny Rabbit
• Bear

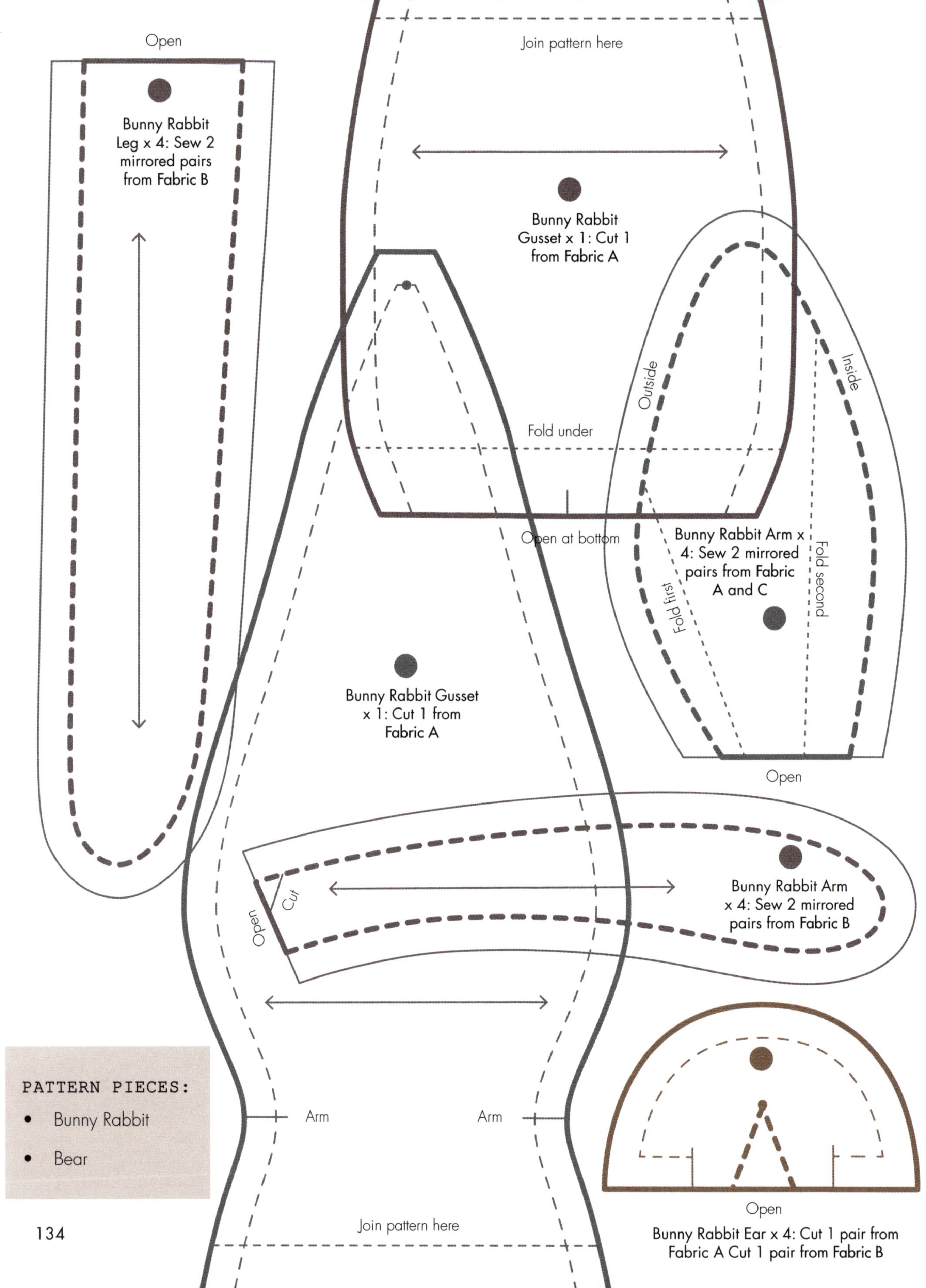

PATTERN PIECES:

- Bunny Rabbit
- Bear

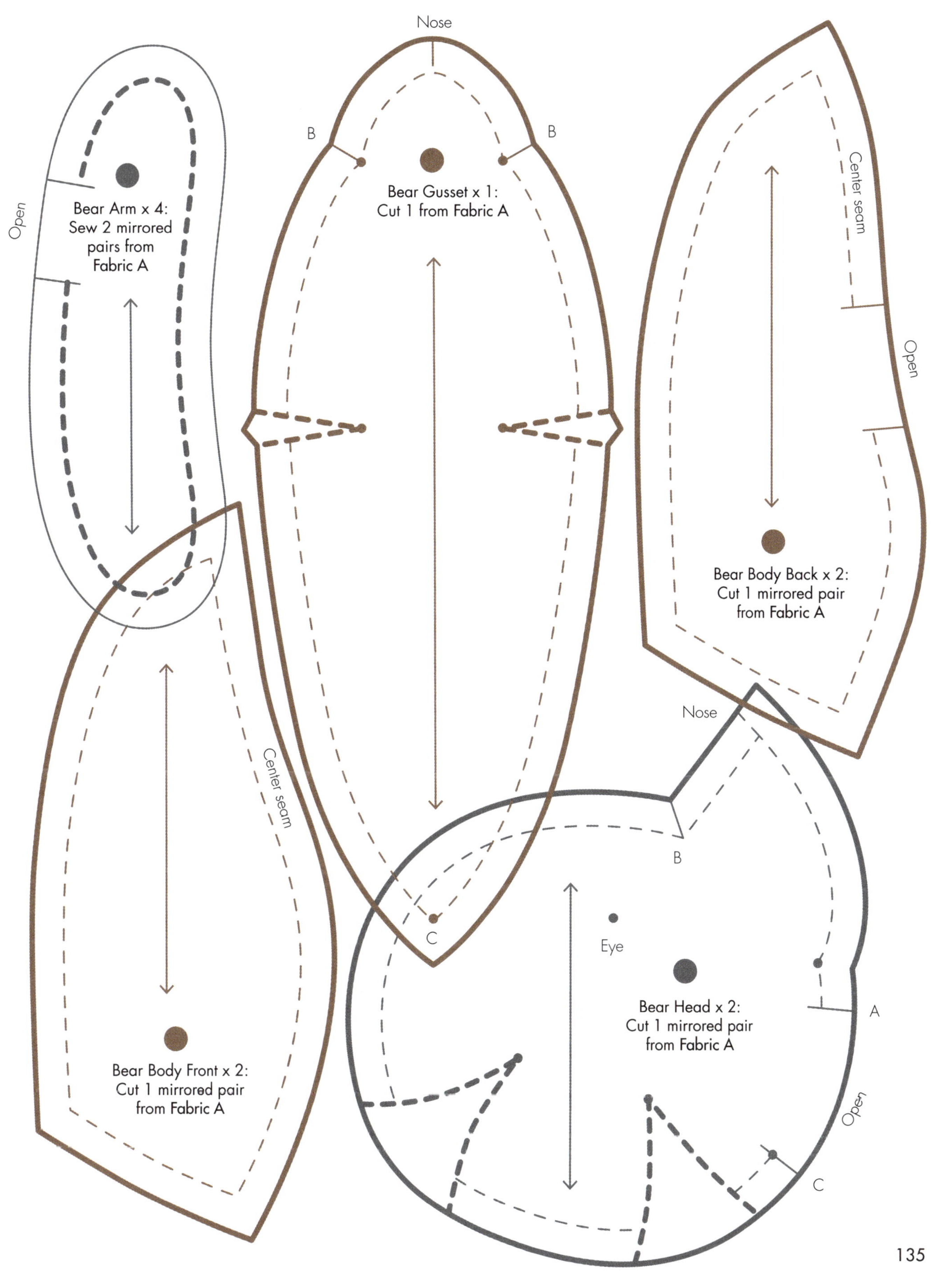
Nose
B
B
Bear Gusset x 1:
Cut 1 from Fabric A
C
Open
Bear Arm x 4:
Sew 2 mirrored
pairs from
Fabric A
Center seam
Open
Bear Body Back x 2:
Cut 1 mirrored pair
from Fabric A
Center seam
Bear Body Front x 2:
Cut 1 mirrored pair
from Fabric A
Nose
B
Eye
Bear Head x 2:
Cut 1 mirrored pair
from Fabric A
A
Open
C

projects

CLOTHING

Okay, now for the fun part! With the clothing and accessory patterns included here, you'll be able to create an entire wardrobe for your lovies. Mix and match and layer them to your heart's content, or keep it simple; even a single accessory can add an enormous amount of charm. The clothing patterns are offered in several sizes to fit the various dolls from Sections 2 and 3, but in reality, because the clothes have elastic neck and waistbands, they can often be shared amongst friends of different species. The accessories also come in several sizes and will fit all the dolls including those from Section 1.

Note that all clothing and accessory patterns include seam allowances.

bow tie

The most dapper of all accessories, bow ties aren't just for fancy occasions.

MATERIALS FOR BOW TIE

- Medium-weight cotton or linen/cotton blend:
  Small bow tie (best for Mouse)
  - Bow x 1: 2½ x 4in (6.5 x 10cm)
  - Knot x 1: 1⅞ x 1⅜in (4.75 x 3.5cm)

  Medium bow tie
  - Bow x 1: 3 x 4½in (7.5 x 11.5cm)
  - Knot x 1: 1⅞ x 1⅜in (4.75 x 3.5cm)

  Large bow tie (best for Section 1 dolls)
  - Bow x 1: 3½ x 5in (9 x 13cm)
  - Knot x 1: 1⅞ x 1½in (4.75 x 4cm)
- ¼in (6mm) ribbon: 16–18in (40–46cm) long

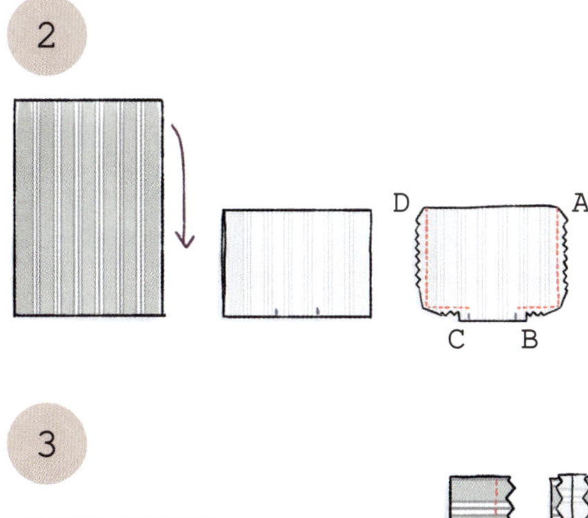

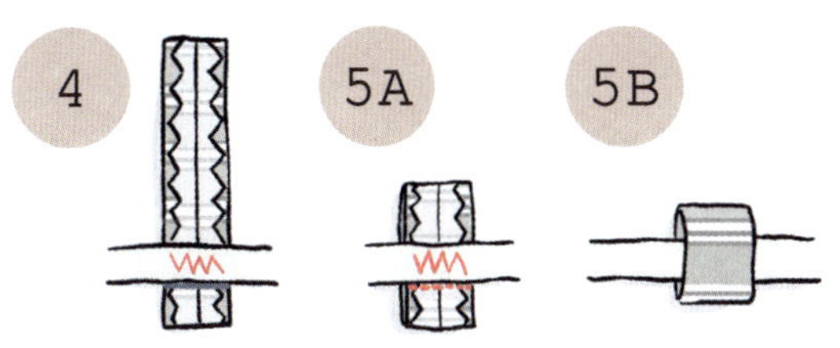

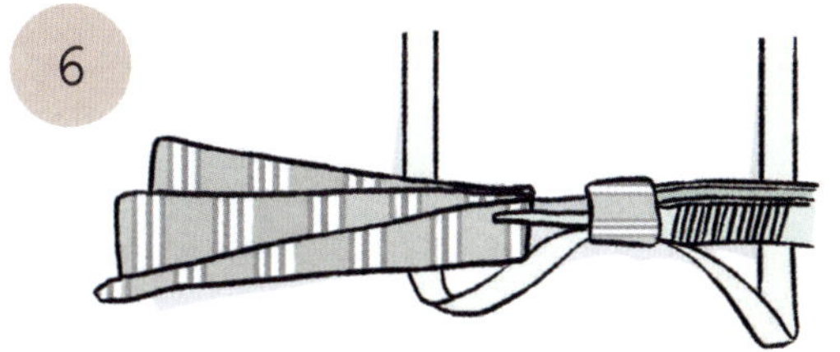

1. Cut 2 rectangles in the relevant size following the guide opposite.

2. *Bow* – Fold Bow piece with right sides facing so that shorter sides meet. Sew from A to B and C to D, leaving an opening for turning of at least 1in (2.5cm). Clip corners and trim seam allowance with pinking shears. Turn right side out and press out seams. Ladder stitch closed (see page 25).

3. *Knot* – Fold Knot piece with *wrong sides facing* so that longer sides meet. Sew along the long open side. Trim seam allowance close to the stitching line with pinking shears. Center the seam and press open.

4. ***Attach ribbon*** – Center the ribbon over the Knot piece laying it crosswise with *wrong sides facing*, ¼in (6mm) up from the bottom edge. Tack well with zig-zag stitches

5. Fold Knot piece in half with right sides facing (the pressed open seam allowance on the outside) and sew across ¼in (6mm) up from the bottom, just outside the ribbon edge. Trim seam allowance with pinking shears and turn right side out. Draw one end of the ribbon through so that it lays perpendicular to the Knot piece.

6. Fold Bow piece in half and then fold the top and bottom in half again so they meet and create an accordion shape. Insert folded Bow piece into Knot piece. It helps to position a pair of tweezers or a hemostat through the Knot piece so that you can grab the folded end of the Bow piece and draw it through. This can be a bit fiddly. Once through, center the Knot on the Bow with the seam of the Knot piece at the back. Tack Bow to Knot with a few hand stitches on the backside to ensure it stays in place.

reversible cape

Lovely on its own or layered over a dress, a cape is an elegant addition to any doll's wardrobe.

MATERIALS FOR REVERSIBLE CAPE

- Pattern piece (see pages 15 and 159)
- **Fabric A**, medium-weight cotton or linen/cotton blend:
- **Fabric B**, medium-weight cotton, linen/cotton blend or try out an alternative material such as minky, plush, or fleece:
  - Mouse: 6¼ x 3¼in (16 x 8.5cm)
  - Dog/Bunny Rabbit/Bear: 7½ x 4½in (16 x 8.5cm)
  - Cat/Fox: 8¼ x 4¼in (21 x 11cm)
  - Section 1 dolls: 8¾ x 4¾in (22 x 12cm)
    - Cape x 2: Cut 1 each from **Fabric A** and **B**
- ¼–⅜in (6mm–1cm) ribbon: 2 pieces 5½–6½in (14 x 16.5cm) long each

PATTERN NOTE

The cape is reversible but the ribbon may not be, so consider this when placing your ribbon.

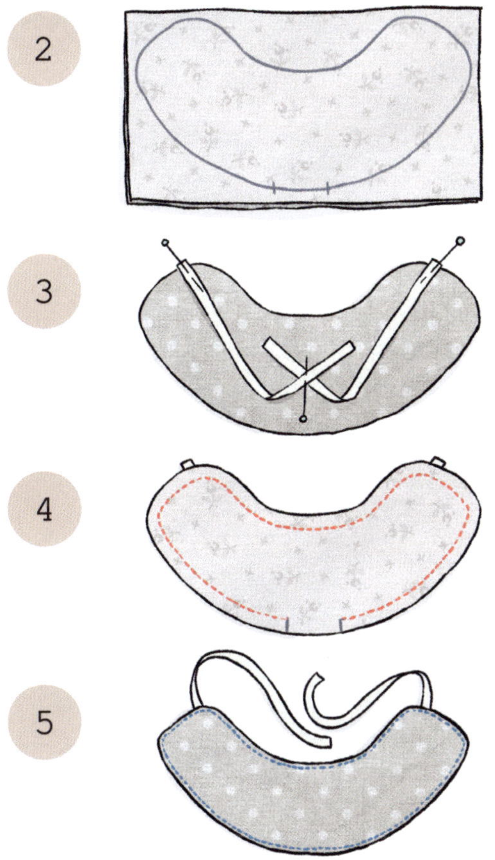

1. *Prepare fabric* – Cut one piece each of **Fabrics A** and **B** following the sizes in the material list.

2. Layer **Fabric B** over **Fabric A** with right sides together and transfer Cape pattern on cutting line. Cut out pattern. Transfer markings for opening to wrong side of **Fabric B** and ribbon placement markings to right side of **Fabric A**.

3. Using markings, lay ribbon pieces on the **Fabric A** piece as shown in the illustration. Let the ribbons overlap the edge of the fabric by a bit. Pin or baste ribbon pieces to **Fabric A** piece along edge, taking care to maintain the correct angle. Fold the length of the ribbon pieces into the center so that they will not get sewn into the seams. Pin to hold them in place, being sure to point the head of the pin towards the opening so that later you will be able to pull it out through the opening before turning the piece right side out.

4. Lay the **Fabric B** piece over the **Fabric A** piece with right sides together. Sew around the Cape, leaving opening for turning. Remove pin holding ribbon in place. Trim seam allowance with pinking shears. Turn right side out and press out seams.

5. Topstitch all the way around the piece ⅛in (3mm) from the edge. This will give us a nice finish, reinforce the attachment of the ribbon ties and close up the opening.

bandana

A classic and versatile accessory that works for cowboys and grannies alike. With the knot tied in front, it can double as a shawl.

MATERIALS FOR BANDANA

- Pattern piece (see pages 15 and 159)
- Medium-weight cotton or linen/cotton blend:
  – Small Bandana (best for Mouse): 11 x 5in (28 x 13cm)
  – Medium Bandana (best for Dog/Bunny Rabbit/Bear): 11¾ x 5½in (30 x 14cm)
  – Large Bandana (best for Cat/Fox/Section 1 dolls):14½ x 5½in (37 x 14cm)
    – Bandana x 1: Cut 1 on double fold
- Turning tube (optional)

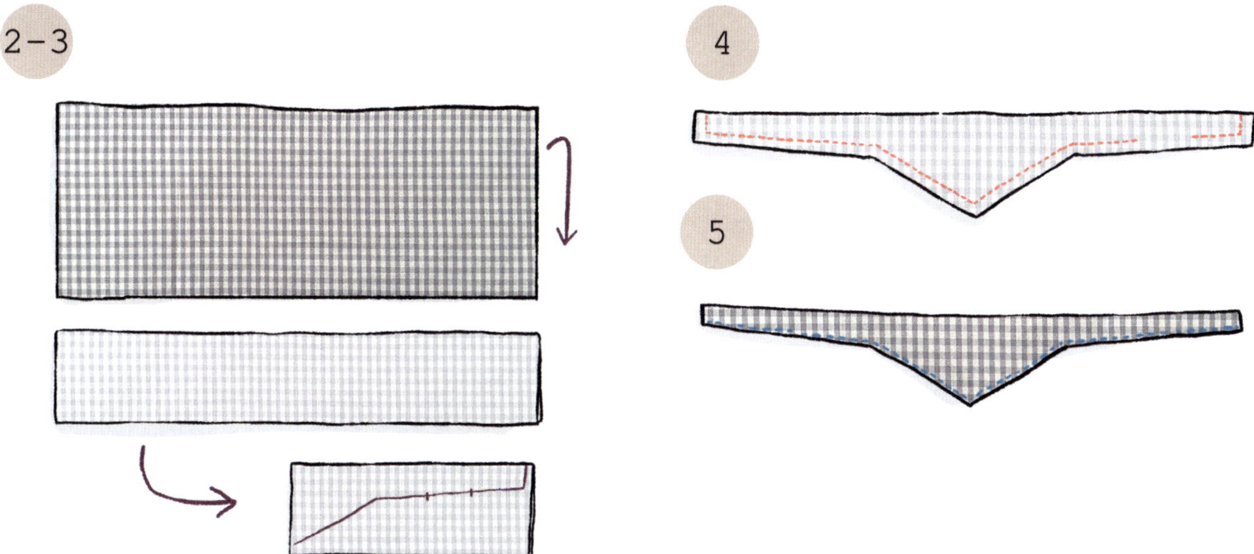

1. *Prepare fabric* – Cut one piece in the relevant size following the guide opposite.

2. Fold fabric in half with right sides together so that longer sides meet. Fold in half the other way so shorter sides meet. Folds must be done in the correct order.

3. Align folded edges with the place-on-fold markings on the pattern piece and transfer pattern on cutting line. Transfer markings for opening. Cut out pattern.

4. With the bandana piece folded lengthwise, right sides together, sew along raw edges, pivoting neatly at corners and leaving an opening for turning as marked. Do not sew along folded edge. Clip corners and trim seam allowance with pinking shears (see page 22). Turn right side out using a turning tube if you have one. Press out seams, taking care to push corners out completely. Tuck in edges neatly and evenly at opening and press well.

5. Topstitch along the bottom of the bandana ⅛in (3mm) from the edge. This will give us a nice finish, keep the seams from rolling and close up the opening at the same time.

neck ruff

The ideal accessory for adding whimsy, drama or a pop of color to any look.

MATERIALS FOR NECK RUFF

- Medium-weight cotton or linen/cotton blend for single layer ruff – see step 1 for quantity
- Or light-weight fabric for double-layer ruff – see step 1 for quantity
- ¼in (6mm) ribbon: see step 1 for quantity

SEWING INSTRUCTIONS FOR NECK RUFF

1. *Determine size of materials needed* – For length of fabric, measure the circumference of the doll's neck and multiply by 3. To determine width of fabric, decide how wide you want the ruff and double it. For example, I typically use a width of 1¼in (3cm) for the Mouse doll and 2¼in (5.75cm) for the Section 1 dolls. For length of ribbon, add 8–12in (20–30.5cm) to the circumference of the doll's neck.

2. Cut 1–2 pieces of fabric to size, depending on whether you are making a single- or double-layer ruff. Cut ribbon to determined length. With the wrong side of the ribbon facing up, mark the center of the ribbon with disappearing-ink pen or with a pin. To either side of the center point, mark half the length of the completed ruff. The length of the completed ruff should be ¼–½in (6mm–1.2cm) less than the circumference of the doll's neck. For example, for a doll with a 7in (18cm) neck we'll want the final size of our ruff to be 6½in (16.5cm); therefore we'll also mark at 3¼in (8.25cm) to either side of the center point.

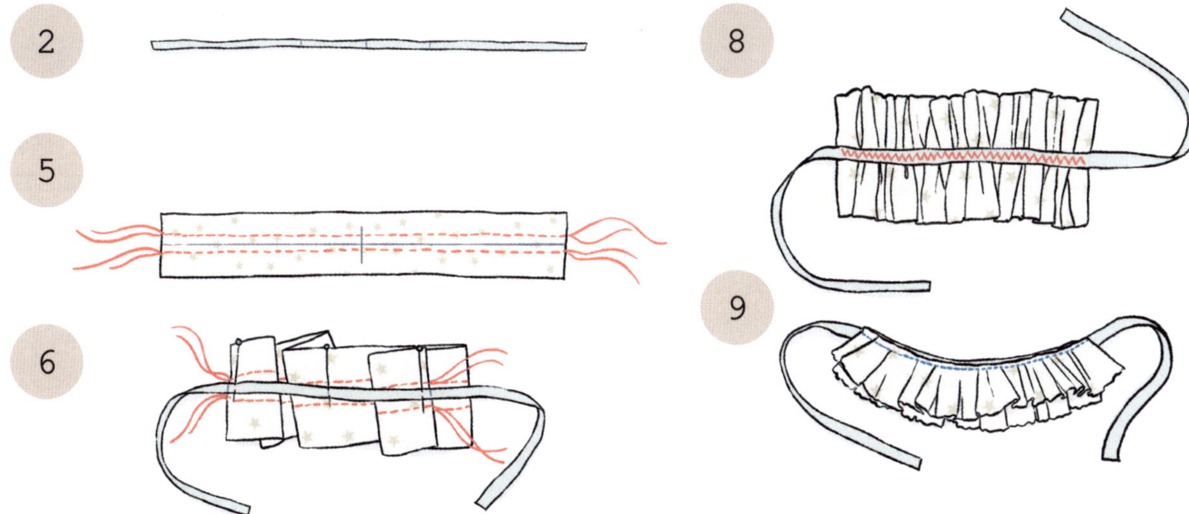

3. *Finish edges* – options include:
   - Leave edges raw for a frayed, primitive look
   - Trim edges with pinking shears to keep them from fraying
   - Use the zig-zag stitch on your sewing machine to run a line of stitching along the edges of the fabric. Match thread color to fabric or use a contrasting thread color for a graphic element

4. For a double-layer ruff, lay pieces with *wrong sides facing*.

5. With the right side of the fabric facing up, draw a line down the center from short end to short end with disappearing-ink pen. Also mark the center lengthwise. Sew two lines of basting stitches ¼in (6mm) to either side of the center line. See Basting to Gather Fabric on page 20. For a double-layer ruff, sew through both layers of fabric.

6. Lay the ribbon wrong side up over the center line between the two rows of basting stitches. Match up and pin the sides and marked center of the fabric to the markings on the ribbon.

7. Take hold of the bobbin thread tails on the underside of the fabric and slide the fabric along the thread to create gathers. Work from each side towards the center until the gathered fabric fits within the marked length of the ribbon. Distribute gathers evenly then pin the ribbon along the center line of the ruff to secure gathers.

8. On the sewing machine, set the zig-zag stitch to a width of 4–4.5mm. As you sew, be careful of pins that may be hidden among the folds. Zig-zag stitch over the ribbon, backstitching at beginning and end to secure. Remove basting stitches, using a seam ripper to help with this, if necessary.

9. Fold the ruff in half lengthwise with the ribbon on the outside and wrong sides facing. The fold should be along the upper edge of the ribbon, making the top layer of the ruff a bit narrower than the bottom layer. Pin to hold. Being careful not to crush the ruffles, topstitch along the edge to keep the ruff folded. Pull fabric apart to create poof.

VARIATIONS

- Make a narrower or wider ruff by adjusting the width of the fabric.
- Make a fuller or more sparse ruff by adjusting the length of the fabric.

dress

With one simple dress pattern, we can make a great variety of lovely items to fill up your doll's wardrobe. Start with a dress and then try one of the variations, like a shirt or a nightgown.

MATERIALS FOR DRESS

- Pattern pieces (see pages 15 and 158) – Sleeve lengths and styles are interchangeable and can be combined with any of the dress and shirt patterns. The only exception is the Mouse dress which can only be combined with the Short Sleeve with Casing option.
- Light-weight fabric – Dresses are best made with light-weight fabric so they don't get too bulky. Cotton lawn, Swiss dot or light-weight linen fabrics work well. Amounts given are for dresses with long sleeves:

  – Mouse: 15½ x 10½in (39.5 x 26.5cm)
  – Dog: 17 x 12½in (43 x 32cm)
  – Bear: 17 x 13½in (43 x 34.5cm)
  – Cat: 17¾ x 14¼in (45 x 36cm)
  – Bunny Rabbit and Fox: 17¾ x 15¾in (45 x 40cm)
    – Dress x 2: Cut 2 on fold
    – Sleeve x 2: Cut 2 on fold
- ¼ (6mm) elastic
- Small safety pin

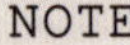

NOTE

The Mouse dress is recommended for confident beginners and up. The small pieces can be difficult to manage and hand sewing is required.

SEWING INSTRUCTIONS FOR DRESS

1. Fold fabric in half with right sides together. Align the fold marking on the pattern piece with the folded edge of the fabric and transfer pattern. Cut out 2 Dress pieces and 2 Sleeve pieces.

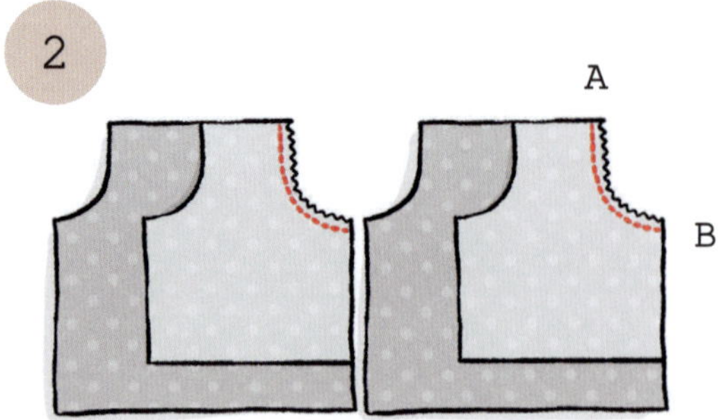

2. Lay Dress pieces next to each other, both with right sides facing up. Lay one Sleeve over each Dress piece with right sides together, aligning them along the curved arm scythe on the right. Sew from A to B for both pieces.

3. Lay one Dress/Sleeve piece over the other with right sides facing, aligning them along the arm scythes on both sides. Be sure that you are matching Sleeve to Dress on one side and Dress to Sleeve on the other. Sew from A to B for each side. Trim seam allowances with pinking shears. Press all four seams to the left.

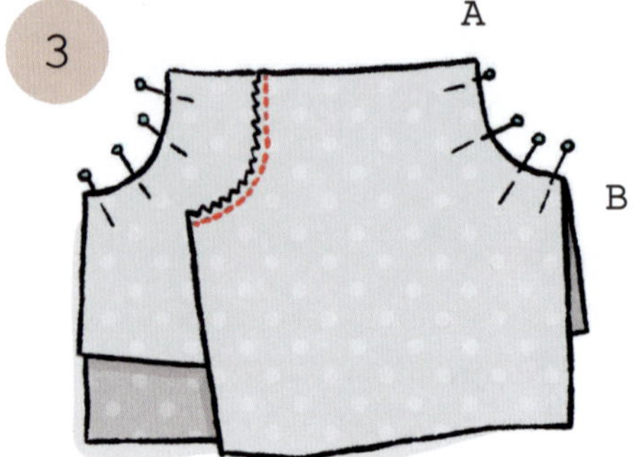

4. *Sew casings* – Fold top edge of Dress/Sleeves ¼in (6mm) towards the inside, then again by ½in (1.2cm) all the way around the neckline. Press well. Sew along the first fold, leaving a 1in (2.5cm) opening for the elastic along one of the Dress pieces. For the Mouse dress, hand sew the casing, leaving an opening. As you sew, be sure that all seams stay pressed to the left. This will make it easier to draw the elastic through the casing later. Sew another line of stitching along the second fold ⅛in (3mm) from top edge of fabric. This second line of stitching gives the casing a neat finish and will help to keep the elastic from getting twisted. Sew casings at Sleeve hems in the same manner.

5. Measure the circumference of the doll's wrist and cut 2 pieces of elastic ¾in (2cm) longer. For each sleeve, attach a safety pin to one end and use it to thread the elastic through the casing, stopping when ¼in (6mm) remains outside the casing. Pin to secure. Continue to draw the safety pin the rest of the way through the casing. Pin elastic in place on the other side with ¼in (6mm) emerging from the casing.

6. *Sew sides* – For each side, fold sleeve with right sides together, aligning armpit seams and raw edges of sleeve and sides. Sew from sleeve edge all the way to the bottom of the dress. (This will join the ends of the elastic at the same time.) Trim seam allowances with pinking shears. Press seams towards the back of the dress where we've left an opening in the casing.

5

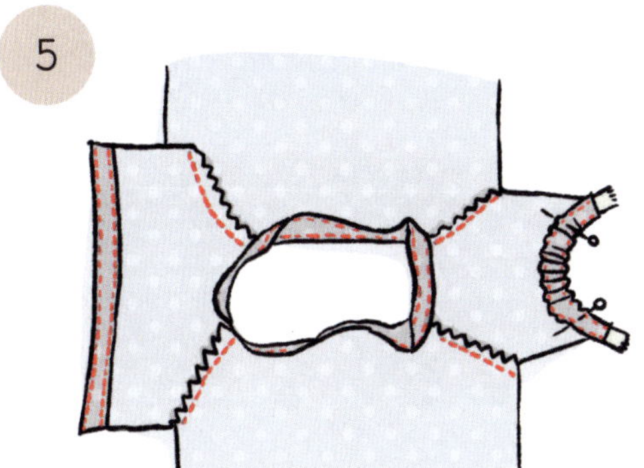

6–8

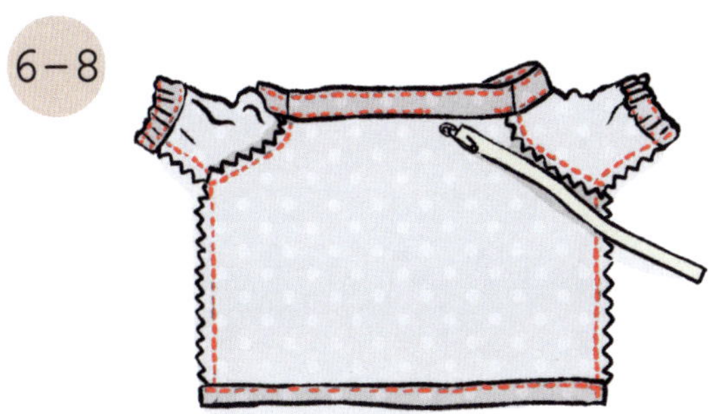

7. ***Stitch the hem*** – Fold the bottom edge of the Dress ¼in (6mm) towards the inside twice. Press well. Sew hem along first fold. Or, if you'd like to add lace or trim, measure the circumference of the hem, add ½in (1.2cm), and cut trim to size. Pin trim right side down over wrong side of the dress aligning its top edge with the top fold of the hem. Leave the last 1in (2.5cm) unpinned. Sew along the top edge. When you come around to the starting point, overlap trim by ¼–½in (6mm–1.2cm) and snip off any excess. For the Mouse dress, you may choose to hand sew the hem as it's so small.

8. Measure the circumference of your doll's neck and cut a piece of elastic ¾in (2cm) longer for Mouse or 1–1¼in (2.5–3cm) longer for all other dolls. Thread the elastic through the casing with a safety pin. Draw out both ends of the elastic and overlap them by ½in (1.2cm), taking care that the elastic isn't twisted. Using your machine (or hand sewing for Mouse dress), sew a zig-zag stitch back and forth a few times over the doubled length to secure it. Let the elastic draw back into the casing and sew the opening closed either by hand or machine. Adjust the fabric so that it's evenly distributed along the elastic at neckline and sleeves.

VARIATIONS:

- ***Dress with short poofy sleeves*** – Use pattern piece provided.
- ***Dress with short non-elastic sleeves*** – Use pattern piece provided. Hem sleeves instead of adding casings and elastic.
- ***Shirt*** (shown on page 119) – Use pattern piece provided. Looks great with a pair of Bloomers and can be combined with any Sleeve option.
- ***Long nightgown*** (shown on page 111) – extend the bottom of the Dress pattern by the desired additional length. Also looks lovely with lace or trim added to the hem – for instructions see step 7, above.

pants

Possibly the most versatile item in a doll's wardrobe, pants look wonderful layered under a dress or, especially with straps added, can make a statement all their own.

MATERIALS FOR PANTS

- Pattern piece (see pages 15 and 158–159)
- Medium-weight cotton or linen/cotton blend:
  - Mouse: 12¼ x 6in (31 x 15cm)
  - Dog: 14 x 6¾in (35.5 x 17cm)
  - Cat: 14½ x 7½in (37 x 19cm)
  - Bunny Rabbit: 14½ x 8¼in (37 x 21cm)
  - Bear: 15 x 7¼in (38 x 18.5cm)
  - Fox: 15½ x 8¼in (39.5 x 21cm)
    - Pants x 2: Cut 2 on fold
- ¼in (6mm) elastic
- Small safety pin

1. Fold fabric in half with right sides together. Align the fold marking on the pattern piece with the folded edge of the fabric and transfer pattern. Cut out 2 Pants pieces.

2. Unfold Pants pieces and lay one over the other with right sides together. Sew crotch seam from A to B on right side only. Trim seam allowance with pinking shears. Press open seam.

3. *Create casing and hem pants* – Fold top edge of fabric ¼in (6mm) towards the inside, then again by ½in (1.2cm). Press well. Sew along the first fold. Sew another line of stitching along the second fold ⅛in (3mm) from top edge of fabric. This second line of stitching gives the casing a neat finish and will help to keep the elastic from getting twisted. For each pant leg, fold the bottom edge of fabric ¼in (6mm) towards the inside twice. Press well. Sew along first fold.

4. Measure the circumference of the doll where the waistband will sit. Cut a piece of elastic which measures ½in (1.2cm) (for Mouse) or ¾in (2cm) (for all other dolls) shorter than the waist measurement. Attach a safety pin to one end and use it to thread the elastic through the casing, stopping when ¼in (6mm) remains outside the casing. Pin to secure. Continue to draw the safety pin the rest of the way through the casing. Pin elastic in place on the other side with ¼in (6mm) emerging from the casing. Remove safety pin.

5. Fold pants with right sides together and sew remaining crotch seam from A to B, backstitching over the elastic once or twice to secure. For Mouse pants, be sure to leave an opening as marked, in order to accommodate the little tail. Trim seam allowance with pinking shears and press open seam.

6. *Sew inseam/inside-leg seam* – Realign piece so that the crotch seams meet in the center. Sew from the bottom hem of one leg through the crotch seam and down the other leg. Trim seam allowance. Adjust fabric so that it's evenly distributed along elastic.

CONTINUES...

VARIATIONS

- ***Bloomers*** – These are best made with light-weight fabric so they don't get too bulky. Cotton lawn, Swiss dot or light-weight linen fabrics work well.

1. To obtain the lovely poofy look of bloomers, we'll modify the Pants pattern to add width. First, add ½–1in (1.2–2.5cm) or more along the straight side representing the folded edge. Remember that any width added will be quadrupled since the piece will be cut twice on the fold. The amount of width you add will depend on the size of your doll and how poofy you would like the bloomers to be. Next, straighten the line of the inseam (from B to bottom edge) making it parallel to the folded edge.

2. Bloomers can be long or short. Measure from the bottom of the doll's body, down the leg to your desired inseam length, then add 1¼in (3cm) to account for the casing and seam allowance. Trace the new pattern.

3. Follow sewing instructions for Pants, but instead of hemming the pant legs, sew casings in the same way we did at the waistband.

4. Measure the circumference of the doll's leg and cut 2 pieces of elastic ¼ (6mm) longer. Thread the elastic through the casing of the pant leg for both sides, pinning at both ends to hold. Continue to follow sewing instructions for Pants.

- ***Shorts*** – To make shorts we'll need to alter the Pants pattern.

1. First, find the point on the inseam/inside-leg seam, ½in (1.2cm) up from the bottom of the pattern, where the line shifts from being vertical to angling towards B. This point determines the width of the pants at the hem. In order to maintain the same width for the shorts, extend the vertical line from the bottom of the inseam to the top of the pattern. The line should be parallel to the folded edge. Next, make a horizontal line from the fold edge of the pattern to B.

2. On the doll, measure from the bottom of the body, down the leg to determine your desired length. Add ¼ (6mm) to account for seam allowance at the crotch. Beginning where the lines intersect on the pattern piece, measure down to the new length and mark that point. Draw a line from B to the new point, then add ½in (1.2cm) to the bottom of the pattern for the hem. Trace the new pattern.

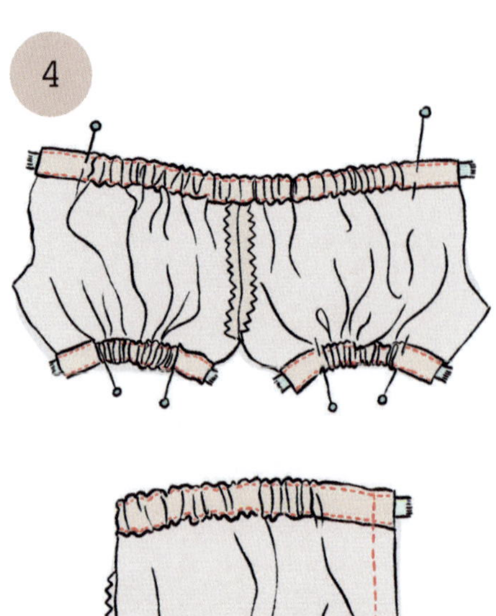

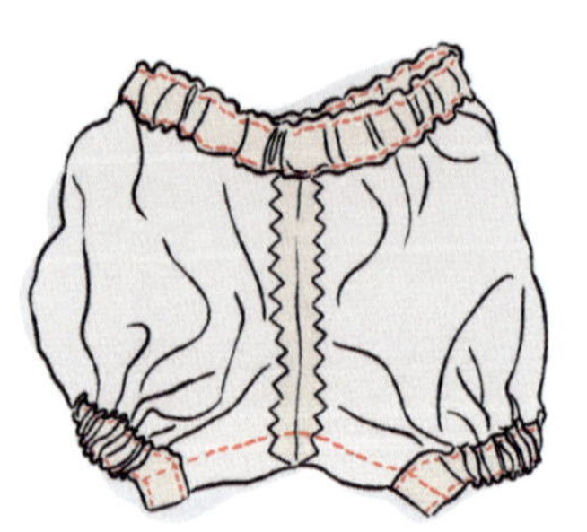

NOTE

Bloomers look great on the larger dolls but Mouse bloomers are not recommended as the pieces would be impossibly small.

PANT STRAPS

Straps are one of the cutest decorative elements that you can add to clothing. They give so much character.

1. To determine length of straps, put the finished pants (or skirt) on your doll. Using a flexible measuring tape, measure from the lower stitch line of the waistband on the front of the pants, starting ½–1in (1.2–2.5cm) (depending on the size of your doll) over from the center seam. Bring the measuring tape over the shoulder then diagonally across to the other side on the back, ½–1in (1.2–2.5cm) over from the center-back seam. The straps will criss-cross in the back. Add 1in (2.5cm) or more to your measurement. You will trim the length later.

2. Cut two pieces of fabric, 1¾in (4.5cm) wide by determined strap length. With right sides out/wrong sides facing for all folds, fold over the short end ¼in (6mm) at one end and press. Fold the fabric in half lengthwise and press. Open fabric and fold in each long side so they meet in the middle and press. Fold along center crease again so that all four layers are stacked and press well. Starting at the end with the ¼in (6mm) fold tucked in, sew along the long side ⅛in (3mm) from the edge, making sure to catch all four layers of fabric. Repeat for other strap.

3. With the pants on the doll, evenly spread the gathers along the waistband. Pin the folded-in ends of the straps to the front of the pants about ½–1in (1.2–2.5cm) to either side of the center seam. Angle the straps as needed in order for them to lay nicely over the shoulders. Criss-cross the straps in the back and tuck them into the back of the pants about ½–1in (1.2–2.5cm) to either side of the center seam, angled as needed. Pin to hold. Note that the straps will be sewn in place at both ends so double check that the straps are long enough to be able to get the doll's arms free and take off the pants. If not, re-pin with added ease.

2

3

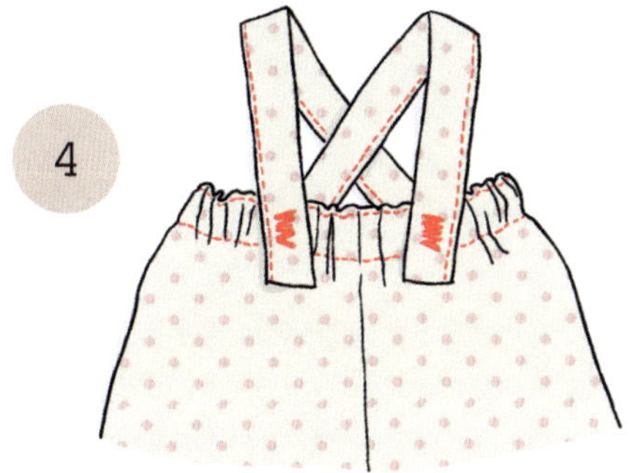

4. Carefully take the pants off the doll. On the back side, hand sew or use your machine's zig-zag stitch to sew the straps to the waistband. Sew back and forth several times to secure well. Trim the ends with pinking shears. On the front side, you have the option to tuck in the straps or leave them on the outside. Attach as on the back side. I usually avoid attaching small items to dolls or their clothing for safety's sake. However, if you do not have safety concerns, you can sew decorative buttons over the stitching or sew on snaps instead to make the straps removable.

skirt

These are so fun and quick to make. Add straps or try some lace along the hem to make them extra special.

MATERIALS FOR SKIRT

- Light- or medium-weight cotton or linen/cotton blend
  - Skirt x 1: see step 1 for size
- ¼in (6mm) elastic
- Lace trim (optional)
- Small safety pin

2

4

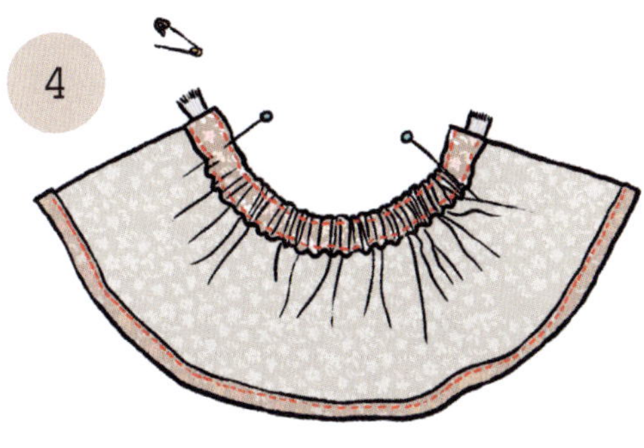

5

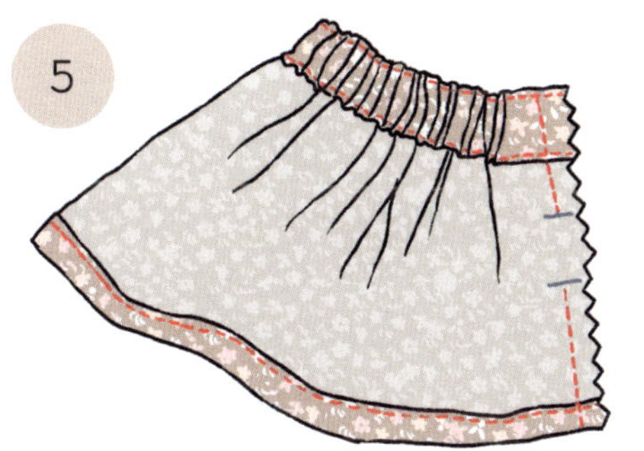

1. *Determine size of materials needed*. On the doll, measure how long you would like the skirt to be, then add 1¼in (3cm) for the casing and hem. Measure the circumference of the doll's waist, multiply by at least 2 depending on how full you'd like the skirt to be, then add ½in (1.2cm) for seam allowance. Cut fabric to size. Cut a piece of elastic which measures ½in (1.2cm) (for Mouse) or ¾in (2cm) (for other dolls) shorter than the waist measurement.

2. *Create casing and hem skirt* – Fold top edge of fabric ¼in (6mm) towards the inside, then again ½in (1.2cm). Press well. Sew along the first fold. Sew another line of stitching along the second fold ⅛in (3mm) from top edge of fabric. For hem, fold bottom edge of fabric ¼in (6mm) towards the inside twice. Press well. Sew along first fold (or see step 3 if adding lace).

3. To add lace or trim, prepare the hem as in step 2. Pin the folds in place, but don't sew the hem yet. Cut a length of trim equal to the length of the hem. With the wrong side of the skirt facing up, lay the trim right side down over the hem. Pin in place, aligning the top of the trim with the top fold of the hem. Sew along the top edge, making sure to catch both trim and hem in the stitching.

4. Attach a safety pin to one end of the elastic and use it to thread the elastic through the waistband casing, stopping when ¼in (6mm) remains outside the casing. Pin to secure. Continue to draw the safety pin the rest of the way through the casing. Pin elastic in place on the other side with ¼in (6mm) emerging from the casing. Remove safety pin.

5. Fold the skirt in half so that raw edges meet. Sew from top to bottom, backstitching over the elastic once or twice to secure. For Mouse skirt, leave a ⅝in (1.5cm) long opening starting 1in (2.5cm) down from the top of the waistband in order to accommodate the little tail. Trim seam allowance with pinking shears and press seam open. Adjust fabric so that it's evenly distributed along elastic.

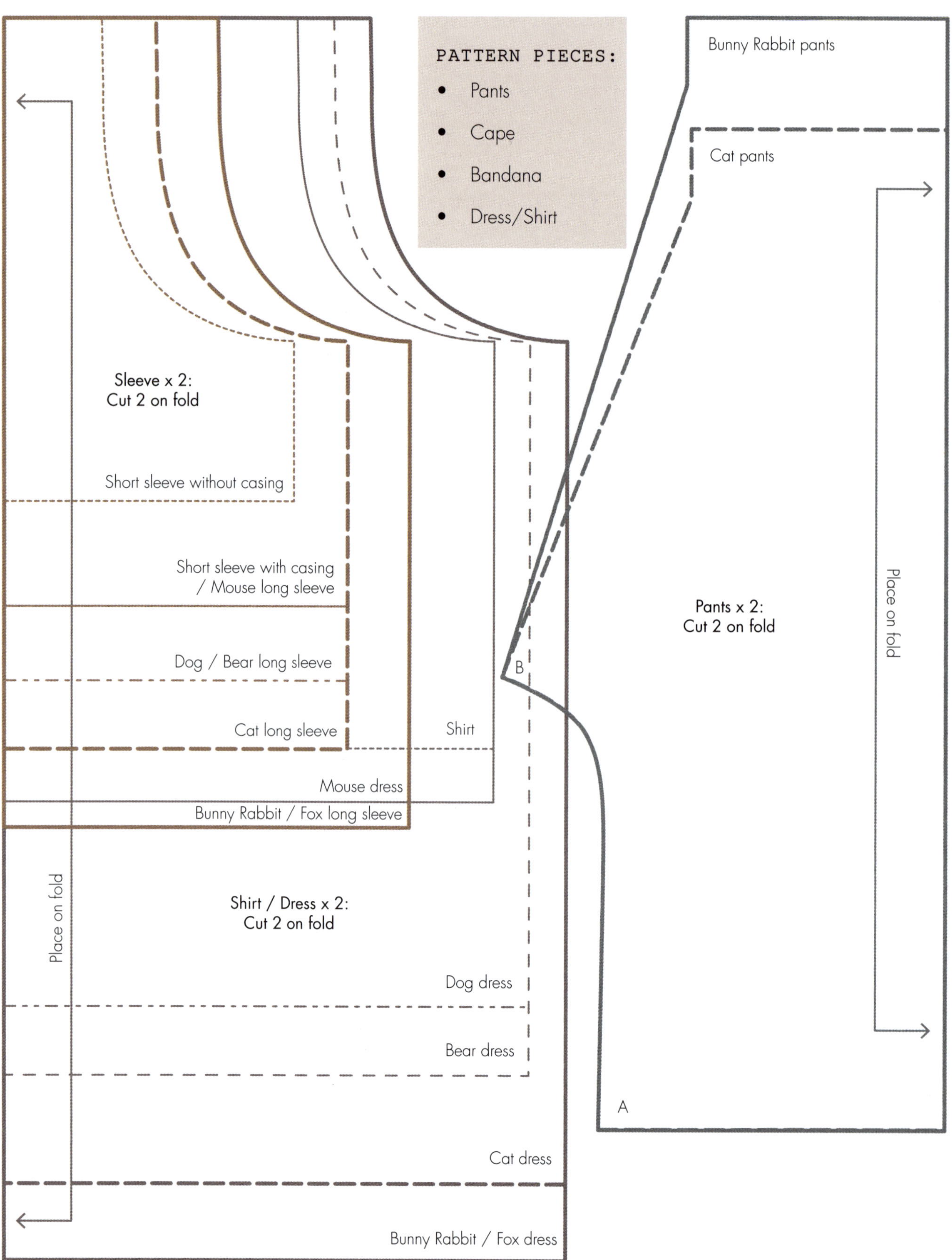

PATTERN PIECES:
• Pants
• Cape
• Bandana
• Dress/Shirt
Sleeve x 2:
Cut 2 on fold
Short sleeve without casing
Short sleeve with casing
/ Mouse long sleeve
Dog / Bear long sleeve
Cat long sleeve
Shirt
Mouse dress
Bunny Rabbit / Fox long sleeve
Shirt / Dress x 2:
Cut 2 on fold
Place on fold
Dog dress
Bear dress
Cat dress
Bunny Rabbit / Fox dress
Bunny Rabbit pants
Cat pants
Pants x 2:
Cut 2 on fold
Place on fold
B
A

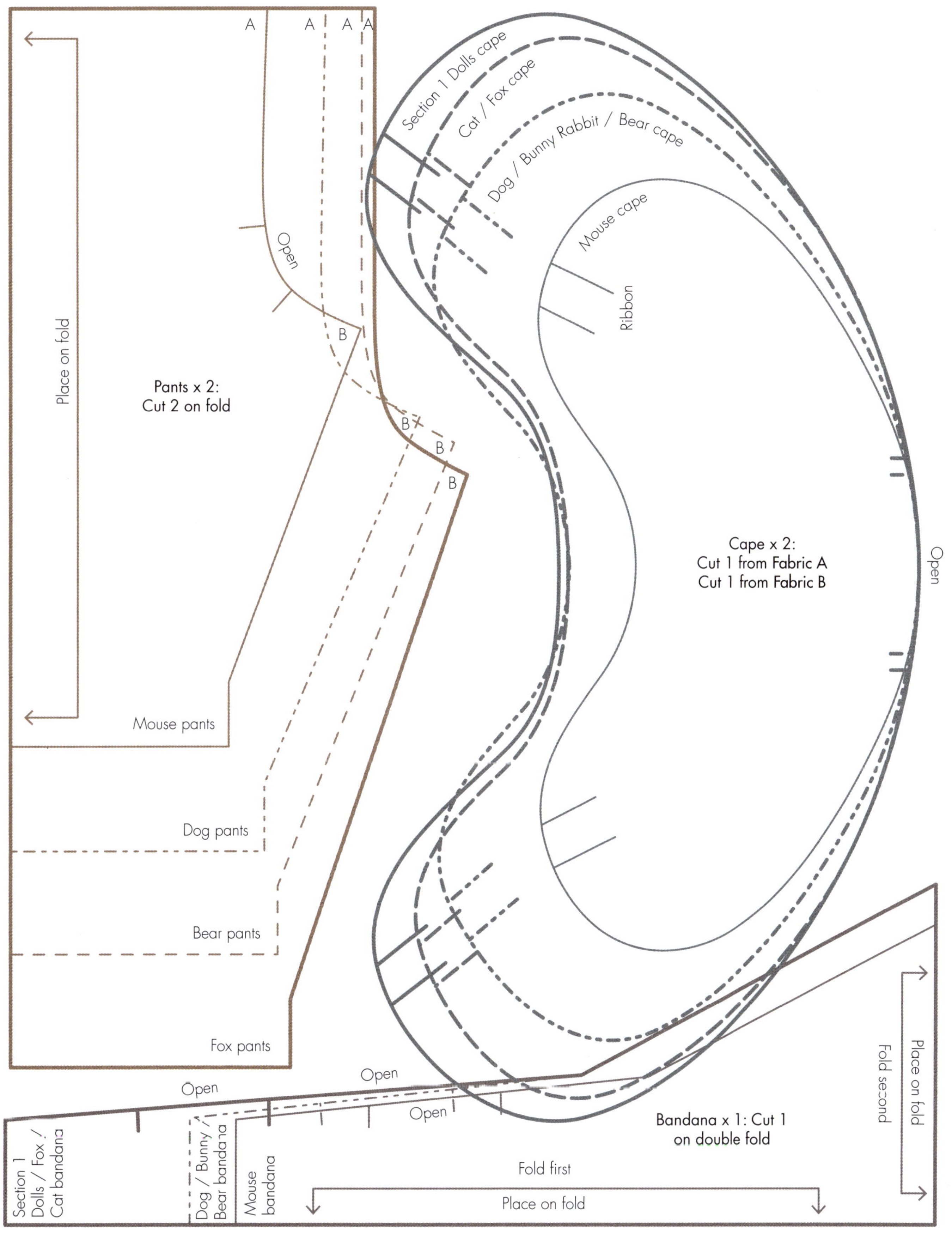

A
A
A
A
Place on fold
Open
B
B
B
B
Pants x 2:
Cut 2 on fold
Mouse pants
Dog pants
Bear pants
Fox pants
Section 1 Dolls cape
Cat / Fox cape
Dog / Bunny Rabbit / Bear cape
Mouse cape
Ribbon
Cape x 2:
Cut 1 from Fabric A
Cut 1 from Fabric B
Open
Open
Open
Open
Section 1 Dolls / Fox / Cat bandana
Dog / Bunny / Bear bandana
Mouse bandana
Bandana x 1: Cut 1 on double fold
Fold first
Place on fold
Fold second
Place on fold

ACKNOWLEDGMENTS

My deep heartfelt gratitude goes out to many people (and dogs) who I'm lucky to have in my life.

To the team who brought this book to life. At Quadrille, Harriet Butt my editor who somehow believed in me enough to give me this wondrous opportunity and Gemma Hayden who did such an extraordinary job with the design. I can't thank you both enough for your patience, generosity and guidance. To Susan Bell for the stunning photography and the ginger and chocolate biscuits you brought for tea. To Claire Robertson for the wonderful illustrations. Thank you for taking this on; I never dreamed in the many years I've been a fan of yours that I would ever have the opportunity to work with you. To Sarah Fisher for all your work on the patterns and getting them to fit in the book. To Charlie Phillips for the styling and sourcing of little treasures. To Jane Cumberbatch for sharing her magical home with us for the photoshoot. And to Minnie for moral support and for gracing the pages of this book. I adored working with you all!

To the many friends who have believed in me and encouraged me along my creative path, with special thanks to Churyl and Lavinia for their steadfast support of this endeavor.

To my children, my original muses, who bring me more joy and delight than I ever thought possible.

To Peter, our rock, who makes it all possible. Thank you for being my partner in this sweet life we have together and for holding down the fort while I worked on this book for forever.

To my mother who taught me about beauty.

To my father who taught me about kindness.

To Conchy who taught me about love.

To Echo who is living proof that childhood dreams come true.

To my lovely and generous customers and the online community who have supported me over these many years.

Thank you.